Towards *A* Free Society
An Introduction to Markets and the Political System
Third Edition

GARY WOLFRAM
Hillsdale College

The McGraw-Hill Companies, Inc.
Primis Custom Publishing

New York St. Louis San Francisco Auckland Bogotá
Caracas Lisbon London Madrid Mexico Milan Montreal
New Delhi Paris San Juan Singapore Sydney Tokyo Toronto

McGraw-Hill Higher Education

A Division of The McGraw-Hill Companies

Towards A Free Society
An Introduction to Markets and the Political System

McGraw-Hill's Primis Custom Publishing consists of products that are produced from camera-ready copy. Peer review, class testing, and accuracy are primarily the responsibility of the author(s).

3 4 5 6 7 8 9 0 GDP GDP 0 9 8 7 6 5 4 3

ISBN 0-07-246397-X

Sponsoring Editor: Tammy Immell
Cover Design: Maggie Lytle
Printer/Binder: Greyden Press

Table of Contents

Preface v

Chapter 1 Introduction 1
Chapter 2 Acquiring the Tools: Demand 7
Chapter 3 More Tools: Supply 25
Chapter 4 Equilibrium 33
Chapter 5 Profit 45
Chapter 6 The Market Economy vs. a Planned Economy 51
Chapter 7 A Just Political System 57
Chapter 8 Individual Liberty 63
Chapter 9 Characteristics of a Free Society: Laws,
          Democracy & Responsibility 67
Chapter 10 Preserving Freedom: The Constitution 77
Chapter 11 Progress: The Basics 83
Chapter 12 A Historical Outline of Western Progress 89
Chapter 13 Lessons From History 107
Chapter 14 The Role of Government & Macroeconomic Theory 111
Chapter 15 Money & The Role of Government 125
Chapter 16 The Individual, The Market System & Society 137

Preface

Each day we go about our business in complete confidence that the rest of society will provide for our basic needs with little thought regarding how it all happens. We do not stop to wonder how the food gets to our table, the clothes into our closet, or how our shelter is provided, all done with no direction from some overriding authority. Yet if we do stop and think about it, it is a great miracle. The market system is a marvel that delivers untold wealth to millions of persons. Societies that do not use a market economy are eventually forced to concede to the reality that only market economies are capable of producing at a scale which allows even the poorest a standard of living above what just a few hundred years ago would have been considered amazing. This book was written for students and thinkers who wish to obtain a basic understanding of this amazing social and economic order.

The socioeconomic order is determined by the rules under which we play the game. This is the political process. But as the French economist Frederic Bastiat notes, it is not possible to develop a science of politics without understanding how the economic system works. Thus, this little book begins with a study of the market process. It then delves into which principles should be kept in mind when setting up a just political system. Next, we'll examine the history of the West with a view toward learning what it is about the West that created such an economic expansion. Finally, we'll look at macroeconomic policy from the viewpoint of the political philosopher seeking the proper role of government.

Towards a Free Society was written as a text for a political economy class I have developed at Hillsdale College. However, it is also meant to be used as either a primary or supplemental text for a one-term introductory economics course, or as a supplemental text for an introduction to political science. While originally intended for first and second year undergraduate students, the text is written at a level that is accessible to a senior level high school social science class. I hope that it will also be read by those who are not in school but who agree with Lugwig von Mises when he says that economics is too important to be left to the experts.

George Munson, who out of his concern for a free society, endowed the George Munson Chair of Political Economy at Hillsdale College, was the inspiration for this book. Without his support, this book never would have been written. I would also like to thank my students who provided much valued feedback over the years, and in particular John Dickey and John Shackleford who graciously provided editorial assistance.

Chapter 1

INTRODUCTION

In this book we will examine the relationship between governmental policies and their economic and political outcomes. We will also delve into the function of the state and the role of the individual in society.

The thesis is simple: much of what goes wrong in today's society occurs because people have not thought very much about how the world works. They are too busy, think themselves uninformed, or simply aren't interested. In the words of Sherlock Holmes, they see but they do not observe. But we will see that it does not require more than average intelligence to make sense of many confusing and contradictory statements—and to recognize that what our government does to solve problems often actually makes things worse. The failure of the general populace to see beyond superficial statements and solutions has lead to the pursuit of wrong-headed policies, even when legislators and members of Congress know their policies will fail.

How the World Really Works: An Example

Many of us are concerned about the violence associated with the illegal drug industry. Drug dealers and their customers shoot one another in the street, and innocent bystanders are often injured. We do not have to cite statistics to reinforce our point: anyone afraid to walk alone through certain neighborhoods of large cities reflects this fear of violence.

Now suppose a politician responds to a poll documenting this fear by introducing "crime-fighting legislation." Our politician claims that this legislation will reduce the number of murders and shootings associated with the drug industry by making it a capital offense[1] to be in possession of a firearm while selling or buying illegal drugs. The presumption is that the new law will discourage drug dealers and their customers from carrying weapons.

The politician hopes to be seen as "tough on crime" and as responsive to her constituents' concerns. At first glance, this proposed legislation seems to be doing the right thing by increasing the penalties for using weapons in the drug industry. But let us think for a minute. The politician has not noticed that the proposed legislation also reduces an offender's "cost" of murdering someone if it is discovered that he has a gun while buying or selling drugs.

---

[1] A crime punishable by death.

1

Look at it this way: suppose the maximum sentence for selling or possessing five grams of cocaine is ten years in prison. Suppose also that the maximum sentence for murder is life imprisonment. Under the current law, a drug dealer carrying a firearm would have an added "cost" for murdering someone beyond the penalty for just selling the drugs. This would discourage him from murdering customers or potential witnesses.

But look at the case under the new law, where being caught buying or selling drugs with a weapon is a capital offense. Suppose a plainclothes policeman catches the drug dealer in the act of selling drugs while the dealer has a weapon. Under the new law, the drug dealer is now threatened with the death penalty. Therefore, murdering the policeman now "costs" nothing additional. With zero "cost" for murdering the policeman, and possibly the death penalty for allowing himself to be arrested, the rational drug dealer will try to kill the policeman. Any potential witnesses will be shot as well.

Now ask yourself if you would sell drugs in the inner-city neighborhoods of Detroit, New York, Los Angeles or any of our larger cities without being armed. Would you walk around unarmed with several thousand dollars in cash? Even if there were a law imposing the death penalty for being caught with a weapon while selling drugs?

We now see that it would not be surprising for the passage of the politician's bill to be followed by an upsurge in shootings of police officers. But few, if any, of the people alerted by the news media to the increase in "cop killings" will associate it with the new mandatory death-sentence law. Indeed, our politician may ask for even more drastic measures to stop the violence.

It may have occurred to you by now that doing precisely the opposite of what politicians initially propose may in fact be the real solution to some of our problems. Later in the book we will see that this instinct is oftentimes correct. After reading this book carefully, you may also find that you often question what your friends accept at first hearing.

Through the Eyes of an Economist: Rationalists on the Bus

In Western Massachusetts there are a number of colleges and universities. Five of these have formed a compact to share facilities and to operate a bus service between the colleges. The bus is free to all students and is often taken between one of the all-women colleges and one of the all-men colleges on Friday and Saturday evenings.

One evening, while riding this bus with a colleague of mine, we were talking to two students about an incident that occurred the winter before my colleague and I had arrived. It seems that one of the buses could not negotiate the rather steep hill that separates the two colleges with its full load of passengers. The bus driver needed to have ten of the students exit the bus in order to make it up the hill.

My colleague and I failed to provide the proper sympathy for the student relating the story, who happened to be one of those required to exit the bus and walk up the hill in a snowstorm. Instead, we became sidetracked over the issue of how to optimally choose the ten persons who must exit the bus.

There are, of course, a number of ways to pick the ten unfortunates who must walk up the hill. Some of those that readily come to mind are:

1. choose the last ten persons who boarded the bus, a sort of first-come first-serve solution;
2. choose those who are best dressed for the inclement weather;
3. choose those who appear to be in the best shape to make the walk up the hill;
4. choose ten freshmen.

You can easily envision a number of other solutions to the problem. Most of these would involve some sense of fairness, usually using a rule that has been established in other contexts, such as the seniority solution (number 4), or attempting to judge which of the students would be least inconvenienced by having to walk. The problem with solutions of this type is that only the individual students on the bus can know to what extent they may be inconvenienced, or what special circumstances they have which might make blindly following a rule of thumb an unfair thing to do.

The solution that came immediately to me and my colleague was to have everyone exit the bus and then buy their way back on. This solution has some appealing characteristics. First, it does not require the bus driver or anyone in authority to judge which students would be best able to negotiate the hill. Neither does it force anyone to make the value judgment of which solution is most fair. Instead, it allows each individual to express his or her value of remaining on the bus. Special circumstances can be taken into account, and students can express their intensity of preference by the amount they are willing to pay to get back on the bus.

Second, there exists a price at which exactly ten persons will be unwilling to pay to get back on the bus. If the bus driver sets the price at $2 and 35 people want to ride, he can move the price higher. If at $3 only 25 people wish to ride, he can move the price lower. There will be a price at which the quantity of seats available will exactly equal the amount of seats demanded.

This market-type solution brings up a number of questions. First, what might one do with the money earned from selling the bus seats? In this case, it really doesn't matter where the money goes.[2] Let's suppose for now that the money is divided among the ten students who did not get the ride. This would compensate them for their misfortune and might seem like the right thing to do.

The second obvious question is: what does one do about those students who forgot to bring their money?[3] It may not seem fair that some students do not have any money with them and therefore cannot express their intensity of preference as well as those who have brought their wallets. One solution to this problem is the capital market: people can borrow from each other. Some students will give up some of their current purchasing power in order to receive the money at a later date. Being friends, and supposing that they will all be back at their dorms later to settle their accounts, the students might simply loan the money to one another at no cost. But, it may be that some students would be willing to loan their money only if compensated by receiving interest, thus being ensured that they will be able to purchase more in the future with the money they are lending then they can at the present moment. This is the purpose of interest, to induce persons who lend to give up consumption today so that the borrower may consume. In return, the borrower will give up consumption in the future when he pays back the lender more than what he originally borrowed.

Let us go back to the suggestion that the seats be chosen by lottery. This seems fair enough; it means everyone has an equal chance of getting back on the bus. People who forgot their wallets might still be able to avoid the inconvenience of walking. However, there is one slight problem with this solution in that it does not go far enough: people should be able to trade their lottery chances either before or after the drawing. This would allow gains from trade to be realized, which is one positive result of the market process. The market process normally allows trading to occur whenever two persons feel they can improve their position through mutual exchange. Let's look at this idea more closely.

In this case, suppose you really would like to avoid walking, and though I don't prefer to walk, it is really of no great consequence to me either way. Under the pure lottery scheme, it is possible that I could get a seat on the bus, and that you might not be as lucky and have to walk.

Given how much money we have, there is a certain value each of us places on our chance of riding the bus. If you value that chance more than I do, there could be an improvement in both our situations if we can trade. Suppose I value

---

[2] The purpose of the price in this case is simply to allocate the existing resource, the supply of bus seats, which is fixed. We will see later that one of the purposes of profit is to increase the amount of resources for the production of a good.

[3] This question is related to the income distribution problem, which we will discuss later when examining incomes in a market economy.

my chance of getting a seat at $2, and you value a chance of winning a seat at $3. You could then offer me $2.50 for my chance, and I would accept. You would be better off because you would now possess an additional chance at getting the seat (which you valued at $3) for only $2.50. I too would be better off because I have given up my chance, which I valued at $2, and for which you have given me $2.50 in return. This illustrates that in the market process, exchange will occur whenever two people value a good differently and when both persons will benefit from the exchange.

We get similar results if we wait for the outcome of the lottery and then allow persons to sell their seats on the bus. The difference now, however, is that the price of the actual seat must be higher than the price of the chance for a seat. This is because we will always pay less for a mere chance than for the object itself.[4] In either case, free-market exchange allows everyone the opportunity to improve his or her position.

In the next few chapters we will further examine the market process. Our method for doing so will be fairly traditional in organization but less traditional in outlook. First, we will look at the demand side of the market, how people make their choices for goods and services and how this information gets transmitted to suppliers. Next, we will investigate how suppliers decide how much to produce and which set of resources to use in producing their product. This is the supply side of the market. Finally, we will examine what happens to the prices of goods and services—and to the amount actually produced and consumed—if changes occur in either the demand or the supply.

---

[4]An economist would say that the value of a chance for something is its "expected value," its value multiplied by the probability that it will be obtained. For example, if the value of the seat is $2, but the chance is only 50% that you will get it, then the value of the chance is $2 x 50%, which equals $1. This is the expected value of the chance of the seat.

Chapter 2

DEMAND: The Basic Concepts

Often in the study of economics you must spend much time acquiring the tools of analysis before you are able to make use of them. Over the next couple of chapters we will be developing some of the basic tools of economic analysis. While developing these tools is often rather dry work, you will find that there are many ways to use the basic tools which will reward your efforts.

Individual Behavior

One of the primary characteristics of the field of economics is its focus on the individual. Other social scientists, sociologists for example, often examine the characteristics of groups and use knowledge of group behavior to explain or predict individual behavior. Economists, on the other hand, do just the opposite and use information gathered from the study of individual behavior to discuss the behavior of entire groups.

Examining criminal behavior offers a good example. One method of looking at such behavior would be to start with criminals as a group. We could try to find characteristics of criminals, such as their age, educational level, family status as children and adults, race, and psychological profile. We then might draw inferences from these characteristics and try to change those we can as a method of reducing crime.

Suppose we find that 60% of convicted robbers are twenty-five-year-old urban black males with an eighth-grade education who have been convicted of a prior crime before the age of fifteen, come from a single-parent family, and are unmarried. From all of this information, we might try to explain how each of these characteristics could contribute to criminal activity, and then undertake policies that might reduce the negative effects of these characteristics. For example, we might reduce the number of persons in the group with our criminal profile by increasing the educational level of urban black males as part of a possible solution.

Economists, on the other hand, would start with a generic individual, and by using the theory of individual behavior would draw conclusions about what sorts of policies would be effective in reducing crime. Let us begin with a little of the theory of individual behavior.

Most economic theory begins with the idea that the best model of how the world works rests upon the idea of a rational, self-interested individual who acts purposefully to achieve the highest level of satisfaction possible while operating under certain constraints. There are many implications that arise from this premise, and we will examine a few of them here.

First, note that we assume individuals are rational. But what do we mean by rational? Logicians tend to define rationality as consistent thinking. Economists, however, generally define rationality as acting in an attempt to get the most satisfaction given one's constraints.

Let us define rationality as "choosing the option that one believes will increase his satisfaction the most when presented with a constrained choice." It is difficult to see the advantage or usefulness of a model that would assume irrationality. One could, perhaps, assume that individuals act randomly, behaving like electrons. We could then develop some probability model about how they might act under certain circumstances. But probably few of us really believe that individuals generally act irrationally. Of course, this depends upon one's notion of irrationality. One might say that I behave irrationally when I return a wallet with money in it which I have found on the street—and which no one knows that I have found. But even situations like this can be fit into the framework of a model of rationality.[5] For example, I might suffer some emotional trauma from the guilt that I would feel if I stole what did not belong to me.

This is what we mean by acting rationally, but what do we mean by self-interest? By self-interest we do not mean selfishness. There is plenty of room in a market economy for Mother Theresa. When Mother Theresa spent her life assisting the poor in India, it did not mean that she was not serving in her own self-interest. As no one forced her to undertake such a choice, we presume that she gained satisfaction from her work. This satisfaction was sufficient reason for her to choose this work over becoming an accountant, earning lots of money, and living in a Chicago high-rise. Americans give billions of dollars to charities in the United States and across the world every year. This does not mean that they are not acting in their own self-interest. As long as they make the choice of giving without being forced to do so, then they are making themselves feel better than if they had spent the money on a new car for themselves.

By individuals being self-interested we simply mean that people will make choices to improve their situation. This can come from buying a new shirt or from giving away the shirt off one's back. In a market economy people do something because it improves their position, not necessarily their wealth or number of possessions.

If we assume that individuals are rational and self-interested, then we can think of a simple rule that will lead us to maximize our satisfaction given any option. That rule is to compare the added benefits from an action to the added costs. If the added benefits exceed the added costs, then undertake the action.[6] Now

---

[5] Robert Frank has a detailed analysis of this kind of behavior by rational individuals in his book, *Passions Within Reason: The Strategic Role of the Emotions* (New York: W.W. Norton, 1988).

[6] This will be discussed in greater detail under marginal benefits and marginal costs, but for now this may be accepted as a general rule.

this action could be anything, for example, buying a pair of shoes, or spending an hour playing Winnie the Pooh with my daughter—and the benefits and costs need not be monetary; I get satisfaction from playing with my children even though they do not pay me for doing it. Nonetheless, it will always be the case that if the added benefit from the action exceeds the added cost, I will have improved my position by undertaking it, and if the added cost exceeds the added benefit, I will have reduced my total satisfaction.

Let us go back to our example of criminal activity. An economist would look at an individual criminal and say that if she commits a crime it is because she has made a rational choice to do so: she must have weighed the added benefits from the crime against the added cost and determined that the added benefit exceeded the added cost. The practical implication of this with regards to public policy is this: if we wish to reduce criminal activity, we must reduce the benefit of committing a crime and increase its cost. After finding out the various benefits and costs of criminal activity, we can then use public policy to attempt to alter them.

This might lead to some of the same policy prescriptions obtained by the sociologist's method of reasoning from group to individual behavior. For example, one of the costs of any criminal activity is the chance of being caught and convicted. If this were to happen, one's future job prospects would be reduced. But if a person is in an area with high unemployment rates, and lacks even a high school education, chances of getting a good job are pretty slim anyway. This is the case with our hypothetical criminal outlined above. Because there is little chance of his getting a good job, the loss of future job prospects will not be an effective deterrent. However, if we increased the person's education level, thus increasing his job prospects, then the loss of these prospects due to a criminal record is greater, the cost of being convicted of any crime and going to prison has gone up, and the person will be less likely to commit crime. Notice that we get the same policy as our sociologist friend, but for different reasons. Thus, increasing the educational level—like our policy maker suggested earlier—would increase the cost of committing a crime and could be used as a policy prescription for reducing criminal activity.

Remember, an economist would say that criminals are behaving rationally given their circumstances and constraints. We can alter their choice of action by altering the rewards and costs of that action.[7] Unless you adjust the benefits and costs in some way or another you will probably not be successful in reducing crime.

---

[7] Convincing the criminal that he should adopt an improved morality is consistent with this line of thinking because by providing the criminal with a moral sense, we will have altered the perceived benefits and costs of criminal activity.

Marginal Analysis

We just hypothesized that rational individuals will follow a general decision making rule: continue any activity as long as the added benefit from doing the activity is larger than the added cost. Such a rule is based upon marginal analysis, something that economists didn't use until the latter part of the 19th century. Let us examine why this rule works.

Economists use the term marginal quite frequently. Marginal just means the next or last one, the unit "at the margin." The insight of economists is that when deciding how often to do something, for example how many movies to see, how many hot dogs to eat, or how many restaurants to open, as long as the added benefit from the next unit is greater than the added cost of undertaking that extra unit, we must be adding more to total benefit than we are to total cost. This means that the net benefit from the activity must be going up. In other words, as long as the marginal benefit exceeds the marginal cost, the net benefit must be going up.

A hypothesis that economists make is that, at least after some point, the marginal benefit from undertaking any activity goes down. For example, consider the shoeless waif on the corner. The first pair of shoes he receives will greatly add to his comfort and happiness. Perhaps the second pair of shoes will add nearly as much to his happiness, as he can use one pair in the winter and one in the summer. But after he gets the third and fourth pair, it is unlikely that each additional pair add as much to his happiness as the pair before it.

While it is fun to try to come up with examples of cases where the diminishing marginal benefit rule, or "Law of Diminishing Returns," does not hold, (perhaps romantic dinners with my wife), it will generally be the case that the marginal benefits of anything decline as you do it more often or get more of it. This can be shown in a simple diagram, as in figure 2-1.

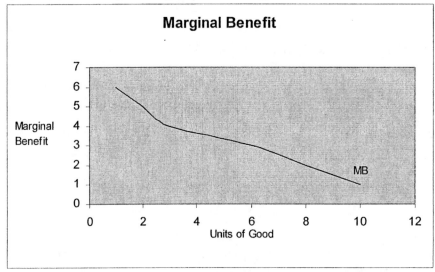

Figure 2-1

Economists also assume that the added cost of doing things increases as the number of times you undertake it increases, at least after some point. In other words, marginal costs increase. For example, if you are producing bicycles, at some point it costs more to produce the next bicycle than it did the one before. There are technical reasons why this should occur, but for our purposes we shall assume it to be true that after some point marginal costs will be increasing. This is shown in figure 2-2.

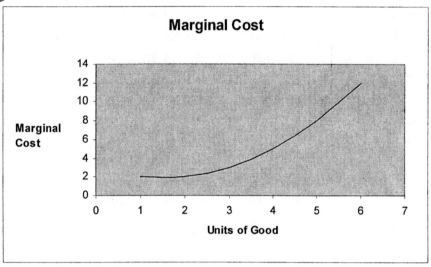

Figure 2-2

In figure 2-3 we show both the marginal benefits and marginal costs of eating oranges. The net benefit from eating the nth orange, say the fifth one, is the difference between the marginal benefit curve and the marginal cost curve. This is shown for the fifth orange as the difference between points a and b in the figure.

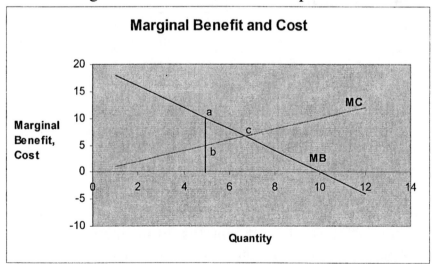

Figure 2-3

As long as the marginal benefit curve lies above the marginal cost curve, additional oranges add to the total net benefit of eating oranges. Past the point c, where marginal benefit equals marginal (at seven oranges), you would be adding more to your cost than to your benefit. The net benefit of the 8th orange would be negative, thus lowering your total net benefit.

Notice that marginal benefits themselves can be negative. After the 10th orange additional oranges actually make you worse off. When you are "full" it means that eating an additional orange will make you less happy.

The total net benefit is the area above the marginal cost curve and below the marginal benefit curve. It should be obvious that this area is maximized at the point where marginal benefit equals marginal cost, or at the seventh orange in this case.

We could also construct a table of total benefits, marginal benefits, and total costs and marginal costs to drive the point home further. In Table 2-1 we list the amount of total benefit and marginal benefit as well as the total cost and marginal cost of going on dates with Mary. We have assumed diminishing marginal benefits and increasing marginal costs. (Although my wife, whose name is Mary, might argue this is one of those instances where the law of diminishing returns does not hold.)

Benefits and Costs of Dates with Mary					
# of Dates	Total Benefit	Marginal Benefit	Total Cost	Marginal Cost	Net Benefit
1	10	10	1	1	9
2	17	7	3	2	14
3	23	6	6	3	17
4	28	5	10	4	18
5	31	3	15	5	16
6	32	1	21	6	11

Table 2-1

In order to calculate the marginal benefit of any unit you must subtract the total benefit of the prior unit from the total benefit of that unit. For example, the marginal benefit of the fourth date with Mary is the total benefit of the fourth date with Mary minus the total benefit of the third date with Mary, or how much that fourth date adds to total benefit. One calculates marginal cost in the same manner, subtracting the total of the (n-1) unit from that of the nth unit.

In this example the number of dates with Mary that maximizes total net benefit is four. Total net benefit at the fourth date is larger than total net benefit at any other date. We can also see that the marginal benefit of dates is greater than the marginal cost through four dates, but marginal cost exceeds marginal benefit for dates five and greater. So the general rule holds that you will continue any activity as long as the marginal benefit is in excess of the marginal cost.

We will use this idea of individuals acting according to rational self-interest to examine the market process in terms of supply and demand. Alfred Marshall, a famous nineteenth-century economist, analyzed the market process by looking at demand and supply as two different blades of a pair of scissors. Neither the demand for a product nor the supply of a product by itself determines how much of that product will be produced or at what price it will be produced. One has to look at both demand and supply and how they interact. We will do this by first examining demand, then supply, and then how they interact to form market equilibrium. All of this will be covered in detail in any principles of economics text. Our purpose here is simply to summarize the concepts and apply them to some policy problems in order to get a feel for how the theory can be used.

Individual Demand

We begin our discussion of market demand for a good or service with individual demand. The demand of any individual for a good or service is a schedule of how much he would be willing to purchase at various prices. We can think of the situation where an auctioneer surveys you and asks how many pairs of shoes you would be willing to purchase if the price of each pair were $90, then how many if the price were $85, then $80, and so on. By listing the prices and the amount you would be willing to purchase, we would generate your demand for shoes.

If we were to draw a picture of this relationship, it would look something like this:

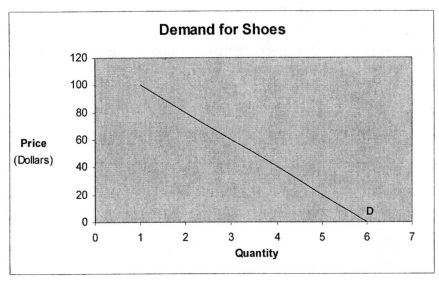

Figure 2-4

There are a few things we might notice right away about the individual demand for shoes. First, the demand is given at—and for—a certain point in time. We might ask how many pairs a week you would buy, how many pairs a year, how many pairs a decade, etc. Thus, we might want to make a distinction between the short-run demand and the long-run demand for shoes.

We also must be careful to distinguish between "demand" and "quantity demanded." Demand refers to the entire schedule of prices and quantities that the individual would be willing to purchase at those prices. In terms of the graph, it is the entire curve. Quantity demanded is how much the individual is willing to purchase at a particular price. Notice that changing the price does not change demand; changing the price changes quantity demanded. This is a mistake often made in the media. You will hear in a news story that the price of oil is rising and therefore demand is falling. This demonstrates that the news commentator does not understand the concept of market demand very well. If the price of oil rises, the demand for oil remains the same, but the quantity demanded of oil falls.

So what does change demand? Well, those things we have implicitly held constant when we surveyed our consumer and asked him how much of a thing he would be willing to buy at the various prices. These include the preferences (also known as tastes) of the individual, the individual's income, and the prices of other goods, particularly substitutes and complements.

People's preferences influence the demand curve. Economists normally take the preferences of the individual as given when examining demand. Of course, an entire industry is made up of folks who attempt to change your preferences. Much of the advertising we see is of this type. You are told that a certain type of automobile will get you a date, or make you seem younger, or that a certain beer is less filling than any other beer. This type of advertising attempts to make you willing to purchase more of the product at the same price. In terms of our diagram, it means that at every price, you are willing to buy more beer than you were before watching the advertisement. This is shown by shifting the demand curve to the right, as from D to Da in Figure 2-5.

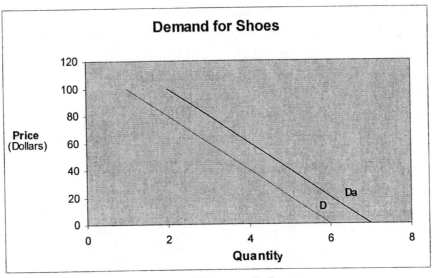

Figure 2-5

A second thing affecting demand is an individual's income. We said earlier that each individual tries to maximize her satisfaction given her constraints. While there are a number of constraints for each of us—our time, our ability to perform certain physical activities, etc.—in the simplest model, the constraint we are concerned about is income. Each of us has a limited amount of income, usually expressed in terms of money (dollars, for example). Given the amount of money we have, we go out and make our purchases. The more money we have, the more purchases we can make (or the more we can give to others), and the greater amount of satisfaction we can obtain. If we are altruistic we may use some of our income to gain satisfaction by giving money to our friends or to certain charities. In any event, the amount of a typical good or service we are willing to purchase at a given price will increase or decrease as our income rises based on whether the good is what economists call a "normal good" or an "inferior good."

Normal goods are defined as those goods that we demand more of as our income rises. For example, we demand more housing services as our income rises. We thus find wealthier people purchasing greater amounts of housing services than poor people, especially in the form of larger, fancier homes. Many goods and services have the characteristic that, given a particular price for the good, we would purchase more of it if we had more income.

An inferior good is a good that we purchase less of as our income rises. This usually occurs because we stop buying the good in question, or reduce our consumption of it, and use another good in its place. For example, hot dogs could be an inferior good for a particular individual. Suppose you earn $300 month as a student assistant at the library. You might find yourself purchasing a lot of hot dogs given your budget constraint. Then you get a job as a research assistant that pays $900 per month. Even though your taste for hot dogs has not changed, and

15

neither has their price, you might instead start buying pizza—or even steak. If we find that you purchase fewer hot dogs when your income goes up, then hot dogs are an inferior good for you. In our diagram this would be shown by a shift in your demand curve to the left, as from D to Da in Figure 2-6. Notice a shift to the left means that at each price you would purchase fewer hot dogs than you would before your income rose.

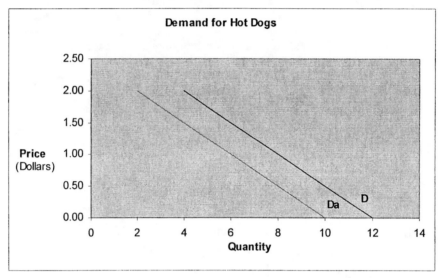

Figure 2-6

Keep in mind that the shift above has occurred primarily because of a change in income.

The third thing affecting the demand curve is the price of substitutes. When asked how many cans of applesauce you would be willing to buy at various prices, your answer would surely depend on the price of canned peaches or whatever other item you might eat instead. Suppose we have mapped out your demand for canned applesauce, and then the price of canned peaches falls from $0.70 to $0.40. Unless you can't stand canned peaches, you would probably change your answers to the questions about how many cans of applesauce you would purchase at the various prices. It would be reasonable to find that you buy less applesauce than you would have before the price of peaches dropped. Of course, this is precisely what the sellers of canned peaches hope for when they lower their price. You are wandering down the aisle and put the applesauce in your cart. When you notice that there is a sale on peaches, you throw a few cans of peaches in your cart and take out the applesauce.

Figure 2-7 shows the situation of substitutes affecting demand. Suppose the price of peaches falls from $0.70 to $0.40. You will buy more peaches than before, but you will now buy fewer cans of apple sauce at every price of apple sauce, since apple sauce and peaches are substitutes. The fall in the price of peaches causes your demand for apple sauce to shift to the left. This is shown in Figure 2-7.

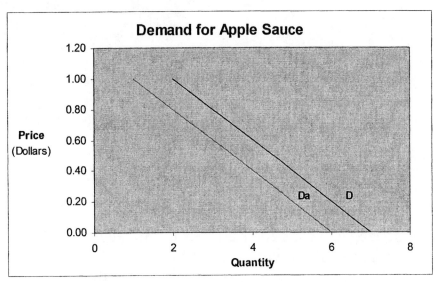

Figure 2-7

The fourth and final category of those things affecting the demand curve is complements. Two goods are complements if when the price of one of the goods rises, the demand for the other good falls. Goods are also called complements if when the price of one good falls, the demand for the other good increases. Going back to our hot dog example, hot dogs and hot dog buns might be two such goods. Suppose we determine your demand for hot dog buns. You would be willing to buy three packages a week at $1 a package, four packages a week at $0.75 a package, five packages at $0.50 a package, and so on. This is represented by D in Figure 2-8. Now suppose the price of hot dogs rises from $1.25 to $3.50 per package. This moves you up your demand curve for hot dogs, decreasing the quantity demanded of hot dogs. (It does not decrease your demand for hot dogs, however.) But now that you are buying fewer hot dogs, you will want to buy less hot dog buns. Thus, at every price for hot dog buns we will find that you want to buy fewer hot dog buns than you did before the price of hot dogs changed. This means your demand for hot dog buns has declined, and thus the demand curve shifts to the left. This effect of the price of a good (in this case, hot dogs) on the demand for its complement (hot dog buns) is represented in Figure 2-8 by a shift in demand from D to Da.

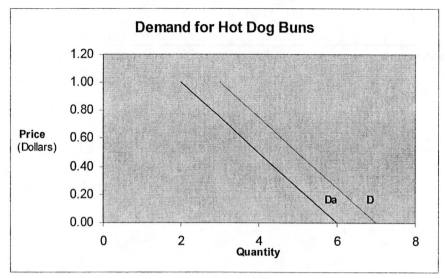

Figure 2-8

To summarize what has been said thus far: the demand of an individual for a product is how much that individual would be willing to buy of that product at various prices. The quantity demanded increases as the price falls, so that the demand curve, which graphically shows the individual demand, slopes down. Each individual's demand curve depends upon the individual's tastes for the good in question, her income, and the prices of other goods, in particular, prices of substitutes and complements. Changes in any of these causes the demand to change, represented by the demand curve shifting to the left or right.[8]

Market Demand

The market demand curve for any product is a very simple concept; it can be thought of as the sum of the demand curves of all the individuals in that market. Thus if you and I are the only ones in the market, and you would purchase four packages of hot dogs at $1.25 and I would purchase three packages at that price, then one point on the market demand curve for hot dogs would be the price $1.25 with quantity demanded of seven packages. We would then do this for all prices and generate the market demand for hot dogs. This is shown in Figure 2-9, where Da is your demand, Db is my demand, and Dm is the market demand.

---

[8] The slopes of the curves may change as well, although the demand curve will always slope down and the supply curve will always slope up.

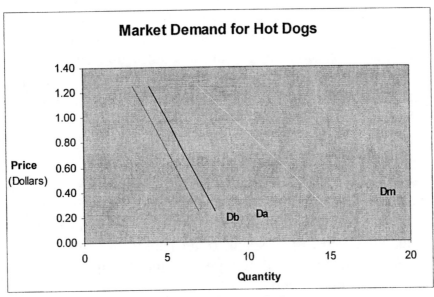

Figure 2-9

Market demand curves have all the characteristics of individual demand curves. That is, they slope down and depend upon tastes, income, and the prices of substitutes and complements.

The market demand curve does not by itself tell us what the price will be in the market, or what the market price will tend towards (neither does the individual demand curve). In order to find this out, we must add the concept of market supply, which we will do in Chapter 3. In Chapter 4 we will examine how market demand interacts with market supply to determine prices and quantities sold in a market. In that chapter we will look at some examples of shifts in market demand caused by changes in the underlying characteristics of market demand and see how this affects the amount of particular goods sold in the market. But first we will introduce the concept of elasticity.

Elasticity

I was introduced to the concept of elasticity when I was an undergraduate taking my first course in economics. While it made sense to me mathematically, I did not see much use for it: I just memorized the formula, answered the exam question about it, and promptly forgot the concept. In my advanced undergraduate courses, elasticity seemed to be used as a mathematical trick to show certain results. This was particularly the case in graduate work. It wasn't until I had the good fortune to become an advisor to the Michigan Senate that I saw how often the concept of elasticity comes up in making public policy. It is a relatively simple— yet powerful—idea.

We just noted several times that demand curves slope down because when prices fall, the quantity demanded increases (and vice versa). But an important question about the demand for a product is how much does quantity demanded rise when the price falls? For example, if I am a senator and vote for a bill that would impose a 4% tax on the price of hot dogs, and this causes hot dog prices to rise by 3%, I know that the quantity demanded of hot dogs will go down. But if I have a major hot dog supplier in my district it will be important to me to know whether hot dog sales will go down by only one-half of a percent or by a 15%. If I know the price elasticity of demand for hot dogs, I can answer this question.

We think of something as being elastic if when a force is applied to it, it responds significantly, and inelastic if it doesn't respond much at all. Price elasticity of demand reflects this general idea of elasticity. It is in the technical definition of elasticity that things seem to get tricky. We define price elasticity of demand as the absolute value[9] of the percentage change in quantity demanded divided by the percentage change in price. This can be written as a simple equation:

$$\varepsilon \ = \ \frac{|\ \%\Delta Qd\ |}{|\ \%\Delta P\ |}$$

where $\%\Delta Qd$ represents the percentage change in quantity demanded and $\%\Delta P$ represents the percentage change in price.

When determining whether the demand for hot dogs is elastic or inelastic, we need to know if the percentage change in quantity demanded following a price change is bigger or smaller than the percentage change in the price. If the percentage change in quantity demanded is larger than the percentage change in price, then ε is bigger than one, and we say that in this portion of the demand curve for hot dogs the price is elastic. On the other hand, if the percentage change in quantity demanded is smaller than the percentage change in price, ε is less than one, and we say the demand is inelastic:

(1) if $\%\Delta Qd > \%\Delta P$ then $\varepsilon > 1$ (elastic)
(2) if $\%\Delta Qd < \%\Delta P$ then $\varepsilon < 1$ (inelastic)

Take a look at the following example. If I know that the price elasticity of demand for hot dogs is one-half (or 0.5), then, based on the formula above, I can tell the Senator that a rise in the price of hot dogs of 3% will cause a decrease in quantity demanded of one half of that, or 1.5%. The algebra is straightforward:

$$.5 = ?/(.03)\ ,\ \text{or}\ \ ? = .5 \times .03,\ \text{or}\ ? = .015,\ \text{or}\ 1.5\%.$$

---

[9] For practical purposes here, absolute value means forget that the sign is negative. Since price and quantity always move in opposite directions the sign will always be negative.

The demand for hot dogs in this case is therefore inelastic. If the price elasticity of demand were two, then the decrease in quantity demanded would be two times the 3%, or 6%.

$$2.0 = ?/(.03), \text{ or } ? = 2.0 \times .03, \text{ or } ? = .06, \text{ or } 6\%.$$

The demand in this case would be elastic.

One of the most useful pieces of information that price elasticity of demand tells us is what happens to the total amount of money spent on a good when the price changes. Total revenue is defined as the price of the good times the quantity sold. If you are the seller of a good, then your total revenue is the price of the good times the amount that you sold. Thus, if hot dogs are $1.25 per package, and ten packages are sold at this price, total revenue is $12.50. Total expenditure is the same thing, only from a different perspective. If you are the purchaser of a good, then total expenditure is the price of the good times the amount that you bought. Total expenditure and total revenue are both defined as price times quantity. Let's now go on and tie this knowledge into what we know about elasticity.

We know that whenever we raise the price of a good the quantity demanded falls. If quantity demanded goes down as price goes up, what happens to total expenditures when price goes up? Recall that price elasticity tells you how much quantity demanded goes down when price goes up. If the demand is inelastic, we know that the percentage change in quantity demanded will be less than the percentage change in price. Thus, for the case of a good with inelastic demand, if the price rises, total expenditure on the good will increase. This is because the increase in the price is not fully offset by the decrease in the quantity demanded. Loosely put, the price is rising faster than the quantity demanded is falling, and thus price times quantity (total expenditure) goes up. Of course, just the opposite occurs if the demand is elastic: the quantity demanded falls faster than the price rises (in percentage terms), and thus total expenditure would fall if the price rose.

In summary:

(1) if price elasticity is less than one, when price rises, total expenditures (or revenue) increases;

(2) if price elasticity is greater than one, when price rises total expenditures (or revenue) decreases;

(3) if price elasticity is equal to one, when price rises there is no change in total expenditure (since the percentage change in quantity demanded is just equal to the percentage change in price.)[10]

Let's put these ideas of elasticity and total expenditure to practical use. Suppose you are the staff director for the Senate committee that deals with federal

_____

[10] It is useful for you to examine what happens in each case when price falls, rather than rises.

drug policy. You are told that the chairman of the committee, Senator Schmoe, is considering a bill that would, if it became law, have the effect of increasing the price of crack cocaine in the United States. Senator Schmoe calls you into her office and asks your opinion of the effectiveness of such legislation in dealing with the nation's cocaine "problem." Think for a minute how you might begin to answer such a question.

Since we are discussing elasticity, you might try to use this concept in your answer. In analyzing this problem you would first think about the price elasticity of demand for crack cocaine. You might try to estimate it by gathering data on prices and quantity demanded, or you might review some articles written about cocaine that have estimates within them. But, even if you do not have an exact number for the price elasticity of demand for crack cocaine, you can make a reasoned guess at whether it is elastic or inelastic. This would entail thinking about whether the quantity demanded changes in percentage terms as much as the price changes.

It is generally acknowledged that crack cocaine is addictive. It is therefore probably true that people who use crack cocaine will not be able to reduce their consumption of it much if the price were to go up (supposing there is no substitute, that is). We would expect that a rise in the price of cocaine of 10%, would result in less than a 10% decline in cocaine purchased by the average crack-cocaine user. This means that the individual demand for cocaine is inelastic.

The next logical step is to think about market demand in terms of elasticity. Since we have already determined that people who are addicted to cocaine are not likely to have elastic demand, it is therefore a relatively good assumption that the market demand for crack cocaine is inelastic. Remember: the market demand for cocaine is the sum of individual demands.

Having now come to this conclusion, you explain this to Senator Schmoe. Your answer to Senator Schmoe's question then follows. If the Senator wishes to reduce the quantity of crack cocaine demanded, then increasing the price of cocaine will accomplish that. How much the quantity demanded goes down, depends upon the price elasticity. Having just explained that the demand for cocaine is inelastic, you can advise her not to expect a large drop in the quantity demanded of cocaine unless her policy will have a substantial affect on the price.

But you can offer her additional information. If the demand for cocaine is inelastic, then increasing its price will cause total expenditures on cocaine to go up. This means that the people who use cocaine will spend more of their income on cocaine, and total revenue for those who sell cocaine will increase. If the Senator wishes to reduce total expenditures on cocaine, rather than reduce quantity demanded, then the bill will do just the opposite of what she wishes. If theft is related to how much people spend on cocaine—perhaps cocaine addicts must steal to get the income to sustain their habit—then her policy would increase theft.

Thus, using the simple concept of elasticity, you can alert Senator Schmoe to the fact that the bill, while it may appear to be the correct public policy at first, will actually cause greater expenditures on cocaine, greater revenue for cocaine dealers, and more theft, to the extent that theft is related to drug use.

There are two important elements to elasticity that warrant further discussion. First, elasticity is defined at a given point along the demand curve. It is possible for elasticity to be different at every point along a demand curve, or to be the same at every point. In fact, a demand curve that is a straight line has the characteristic that, while its slope is constant, elasticity differs at every point. For a particular demand curve called a rectangular hyperbola, elasticity is equal to one at ever point. Thus, when discussing whether demand is inelastic or elastic, we usually speak of it as being "elastic in the relevant range," or "inelastic in the relevant range." This means that in the area of the curve under discussion, the elasticity is elastic or inelastic.

It is also important to note that demand curves are more elastic the longer the length of time individuals have to respond to a price change. For example, if the price of gasoline doubled, in the short run you would probably not reduce your gasoline consumption by one half. However, over the course of a year or two you might buy a car that gets better gas mileage, or even move closer to where you work. So long run demand curves are generally more elastic than short run demand curves.

Why should you care about concepts such as elasticity? Perhaps you will not be an advisor to a United States senator, but you are a citizen, and probably are, or will be, a taxpayer. If citizens are not able to judge the efficacy of government actions independently of the opinions of the media and the viewpoints of their elected officials, then governmental policies may produce exactly the opposite result of what the citizens, or even the politicians espousing these policies, would really want.

Chapter 3

SUPPLY

In this chapter we will add the other blade of Alfred Marshall's scissors: supply. We will then be able to make sense of a number of everyday puzzles and to form sensible opinions about public policy. But first, we must introduce another concept that will seem intuitive to you, but which until now you may not have had a name for. That concept is opportunity cost.

Opportunity Cost

Suppose you are at a party and have been there for three hours and now you have to get back to studying. Then the party host announces that pizzas are arriving, and that they are free. What the host really means is that he is not going to charge you for the pizza. But are they really free to you? Most people would say yes and think no further. There is, however, a cost to you for staying and eating, and that cost is the value of whatever else you would be doing with your time if you did not stay to eat pizza.

If you valued studying for your exam at $3 per hour, and you would take an hour to eat and mingle (you would not want to shoot out of the party seconds after devouring the last piece of pizza and risk not getting invited back), then the pizza really costs you $3. An economist would say that the opportunity cost of the pizza is the $3 value placed on the time you would have spent somewhere else.

We define opportunity cost more generally as whatever you must give up in order to get something. It is the value of your next best opportunity, and that is, of course, why it is called opportunity cost. Individuals often have an innate sense of opportunity cost and make rational choices based on this. But sometimes they do not. And many times government policies are made to sound beneficial when they really would not be if you took opportunity cost into account. Let's look at a couple more examples, and then we will see how opportunity cost fits into an analysis of supply.

As indicated in our free-pizza situation, people often overlook the opportunity cost of their time. When deciding whether or not to spend four years at college, one usually considers the cost of tuition, books, room and board, and other out-of-pocket expenses. But one should also consider the opportunity cost of your time. If you could earn $20 per hour in an automobile factory straight out of high school, then in addition to the other expenses, the opportunity cost of a year of college would include what you could have earned in the automobile factory. Since there are about two thousand hours in a work year, you would be giving up $40,000 per year to attend college. Now you might earn some money during the summer of your school year. Nonetheless, the opportunity cost of going to school would still be considerable. It would not be surprising to discover that a large number of highly paid factory workers did not go to college. It wouldn't necessarily be that they were uninterested in higher education or did not have the grades to get into college. It is simply the case that the opportunity cost of college was higher for them than for teenagers who did not have such job opportunities available to them.

This also explains why certain outstanding college football and basketball players do not complete college. They are able to earn sufficiently high salaries in professional sports such that the opportunity cost of finishing their education is too high. If we remember the old expression, "I had something better to do," we can remember that we should always examine the opportunity cost of our time when making a decision.

Let's apply the idea of opportunity cost to public policy. Public officials often do not include the opportunity cost of our tax dollars when espousing the benefits of a program. Suppose that Representative Pacbucks has a program that funds early childhood education. This program will cost $50 million in tax dollars. The representative explains all the good aspects of the program and says that it will solve a number of social problems about which we are all concerned. But even if the program is effective in solving some of these social problems, we still do not know if we should support it until we think about what else the $50 million could be used for. As an example, by spending $50 million on the early childhood program we cannot spend the same $50 million on prenatal care for the poor, or on a new hospital for cancer patients. We must also think about what the $50 million could do if it remained in the pockets of taxpayers who might buy more milk for their children, or purchase more housing services.

The economist Henry Hazlitt pointed out over fifty years ago that when government undertakes a project, for example, building a bridge, the project is visible and can be appreciated.[11] What is not seen is what we are calling the opportunity cost of the project, those items that were not built because the resources that went into the bridge were diverted from other uses. The point is that resources used for one thing cannot be used for something else. When judging whether we support a particular public project we must keep in mind the opportunity cost of the resources which will be used up in carrying out that project. It is important to recognize these forgone opportunities.

---

[11] See his little book, *Economics in One Lesson* (New York: Arlington House, 1979), originally published by Harper and Bros. in 1946.

Obtaining Resources

In order to get the resources to produce something in a market economy you must bid those resources away from whatever else they might be used for. This applies to non-human resources, like cement and steel, and to human labor services as well. In the terminology introduced above, you must pay the resource owner his opportunity cost.

If I own ten tons of steel and you wish to use that steel to build an apartment complex, then you must pay me at least as much for my steel as I can get from anyone else who also wishes to buy it. The opportunity cost of selling you my steel is what I could have received for the steel from another purchaser. This is also true of my labor services. If I can earn $8 per hour at the local car wash, and you wish to have me work in your restaurant, the opportunity cost of working for you is the $8 per hour I could earn at the car wash. You must pay me at least $8 per hour to work at your restaurant.

Persons who supply goods and services to the economy must therefore pay the owner of the resource the opportunity cost the resource in order to obtain it for the production process. However, they cannot pay more for a resource than the value of the added product that results from using that resource. If they did, they would not survive long in a market economy. For example, if you were to hire me at $8 per hour, and I produced only $4 per hour worth of services, then you would either have to lower my wage, fire me, or go out of business.

There are two results from this phenomenon of having to pay the opportunity costs of resources. First, we know that in a market economy resources are put to their most valued use since owners of a resource can freely sell the resource to the highest bidder. If you offer me $10 per ton for my steel, you must be getting at least $10 per ton of product out of it; otherwise you'd go out of business. If you are the highest bidder for my steel, I will sell it to you and it could have had no higher valued use in society. If it did, someone would have bid more than the $10.

Second, consumers determine the value of resources and thus the income of resource owners (this includes the wages of individuals). This is because producers cannot pay a resource owner more than the amount that consumers value the added product or service that results from the use of any resource. For example, if you are a buggy whip maker, and I hire you to make buggy whips in my factory, and consumers decide they no longer want to purchase buggy whips, I cannot continue to hire you at the wage we originally agreed upon. The lack of consumer demand for the product that you produce and I sell will lower both our incomes. This, of course, is true for all resources and their owners. As soon as consumers reduce their demand for a good or service, the earnings of all resources in that industry

27

will decline. Likewise, when consumers increase their demand for a product, the earnings of all resource owners in that industry will increase.

As another example, suppose I were paying you $10 per hour to work in my buggy whip factory, and by hiring you the company would be making five more buggy whips per hour. If the price of buggy whips were $3, it would make sense for me to hire you, since I would be taking in an extra $15 per hour. However, if the price of buggy whips fell to $1, then I would be paying you $10 per hour and I would only be taking in an extra $5 per hour for your work. It would not take long for me to go out of business under such circumstances. The only way for me to be able to continue employing you would be for your wage to fall or for you to work more productively so that you were adding as much to my revenue as your wages were costing me.

Supply Curve

Having looked at the ideas of opportunity cost and obtaining resources, we can now use the same concepts for supply that we did for demand. We can imagine an auctioneer asking producers of a particular good how many units they would be willing to produce at various prices. We could then create a supply curve in the same way we fashioned a demand curve. Pick a given price, and see how many units would be offered for sale; pick another price and see how many units would be offered, and continue over a wide range of prices. What would the shape of the supply curve look like?

First, it would slope upward because in order to produce more of a good I must obtain more resources. As my fellow producers and I try to get more of a resource, say steel, we will have to obtain it from resource owners who have higher and higher opportunity costs. In order to get the first ton of steel we may get it from a small dealer in town who doesn't have many places to market his steel. But as we try to get more and more, we may have to get some from producers who have been offered high prices from the auto industry. Or think of trying to get a babysitter on New Year's Eve. If you need one babysitter, you might be able to find someone who doesn't have a girlfriend, has no hope of getting a date, and would be just as willing to watch your TV as their own. But if you need ten babysitters, you might have to pay someone who would be giving up a splendid night on the town which they value at $100.

There are other more technical reasons why we would expect producers to be willing to offer more goods and services at higher prices than they would at lower prices. One reason is that as we add more of one resource to a fixed supply of that resource, the additional product from the added resource gets smaller. For example, if I have three people working in my plant and I add a computer, I may get $3000 in added product. When I add a second computer I may also get $3000

28

of added product. But as I add a third and a fourth computer, additional computers will add less and less to total product. This is known as the assumption of diminishing marginal product and it is a primary reason that we get the assumption of increasing marginal costs discussed earlier. As with other concepts, this is discussed more fully in any introductory textbook, but for our purposes we may assume that marginal product eventually declines and marginal costs eventually increase.

Using our general rule that we continue to do things as long as the marginal benefit exceeds the marginal cost, I will continue to produce more of a good as long as the marginal cost is less than the price. This means that the supply curve for a firm will be its marginal cost curve. Since marginal cost rises as the number of units of the output rises, at least after some point, the firm's supply curve will slope upwards, as in Figure 3-1.

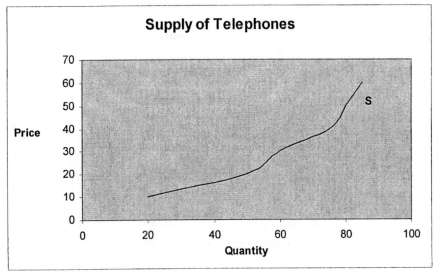

Figure 3-1

Here we have the market supply curve for telephones. At $20 per phone, producers would supply fifty phones, at $40 they would supply seventy-five phones, and so on.

Just as with demand, we want to be careful of the difference between "supply" and "quantity supplied." Supply refers to the whole schedule or curve, whereas quantity supplied is the amount that would be offered at a particular price. Thus, there is a quantity supplied for each price, and the entire set of prices and quantities supplied is referred to as supply.

As we did with demand curves, we need to examine what affects the supply curve, namely the price of inputs, technology, and the number of producers.

The first major determinant of supply is the price of inputs. Inputs are those resources that go into the production of any given product. Recall that the demand curve only shows the price of a good and the quantity demanded. Anything else that affects the demand for a good other than price is shown by a shift in the demand curve. The same holds true for the supply curve. Our next logical question, then, is how do inputs affect the supply curve? As we noted above when thinking about why supply curves slope up, an important determinant of how much of any given thing will be offered to the market at any given price is the price of resources used to produce the good or service. For example, since oil is used to produce gasoline, if the price of oil goes from $25 per barrel to $40 per barrel, then the amount of gasoline that a producer is willing to sell at each price (and willing to produce) will surely be less than before the price increase. A general rule can be stated here: as the price of an input goes up, producers are willing to produce less of a product at every price, and thus the supply curve for the product containing that input shifts left. This is indicated by a shift of the supply curve from S to S' in figure 3-2.

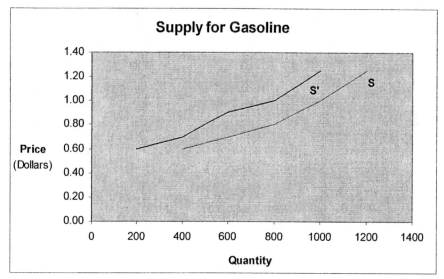

Figure 3-2

At oil prices of $25 per barrel, gasoline producers were willing to sell twelve hundred gallons at $1.25, one thousand gallons at $1 per gallon, nine hundred gallons at $0.90 per gallon, et cetera. This is indicated by supply curve S. When the price of oil rises to $40 per barrel, then producers of gasoline will only offer one thousand gallons at $1.25 per gallon, eight hundred gallons at $1, and six hundred gallons at $0.90. This is shown in Figure 3-2 by shifting the supply curve to S'.

If the price of an input fell—perhaps if oil went to $20 per barrel in our example—then the supply curve for gasoline would shift to the right. At every price producers would be willing to supply more than before the fall in the price of the input.

Another primary determinant of supply is the technology of production. Technology of production determines how much of the output can be produced for a given input. One of the major changes that occurred during the Industrial Revolution involved techniques of production which allowed goods to be produced at substantially lower cost than had been previously possible. When the production techniques change so a good can be produced at lower cost (often by using cheaper or fewer inputs for the same output), then we would expect producers to be willing to supply more of a good at any given price. Again, this is seen as a shift in the supply curve to the right.

The third major determinant of supply is the number of producers in the market. When our hypothetical auctioneer was asking how much would be produced at a given price, he was asking the question of a fixed number of producers. But suppose the number of producers in the market increased. Then, of course, for each price we would get a larger quantity supplied. This is shown by a shift in the supply curve to the right. If the number of producers in the market declined, the quantity supplied at each price would decline and would be shown by a shift in the supply curve to the left.

Having discussed the elementary points of demand and supply, and the factors that affect both curves, the next step is to put the two concepts together and tackle the concept of market equilibrium. This is exactly what we will do in the next chapter.

Chapter 4

EQUILIBRIUM

Now that we have the basic tools of market analysis at our disposal, demand and supply curves, let us put them to use. Neither the demand curve nor the supply curve by themselves can tell us what the market price for a product will be. Nor can either curve tell us how much of any product will be sold in the market. But by putting the two curves together, we can get an idea what the market price and quantity will be.

Putting Demand and Supply Together

In Figure 4-1, we have both the demand and supply curves. Notice that, as we have pointed out before, the demand curve slopes down and the supply curve slopes up. This means that as prices fall a greater quantity is demanded and a smaller quantity is supplied. Notice also that there is one point where the demand and supply curves intersect. It is this point that is of primary interest.

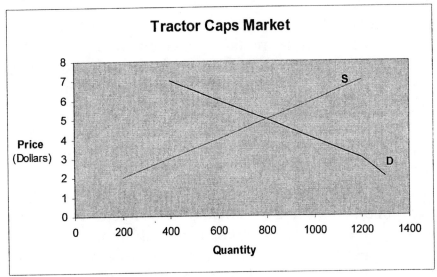

Figure 4-1

What is the graph telling us at the point where the demand and supply curves intersect? Suppose that this is the demand and supply of tractor caps. At $5 we see that the quantity demanded of tractor caps is 800, and that the quantity supplied of tractor caps is 800. There are no people out there who want tractor caps for $5 that can't find them, and there are no producers who have a big stock of tractor caps sitting around that they had hoped to sell for $5. This is what economists call market equilibrium. Everyone in our story has had their expectations satisfied.

Suppose we look at the $4 price. Moving down the demand curve, we find at this price that the quantity demanded of tractor caps is 1000. However, we also find that we are moving down the supply curve, and that the quantity supplied of tractor caps is 600. This clearly is not a happy situation, at least for consumers. There will be a good number of people who hoped to buy tractor caps for $4 who will be frustrated and unable find them. There will be "excess demand." This situation regularly occurs in societies where prices are not set by the market, the same places where one sees people standing in line for goods but unable to obtain the amount they wish to purchase for the price being asked.

Can such a situation last in a free market? Let us think what is likely to happen with our tractor cap situation. Notice that there will be a large number of people willing to buy tractor caps at a price higher than $4. We already noticed that at $5 consumers would be willing to purchase 800 tractor caps. Some of these people will offer producers more than the $4, perhaps $4.50. This will have two effects. First, the producers will see that they can get more than $4 for tractor caps. They will offer more tractor caps for sale at a higher price, thereby moving up the supply curve. Second, fewer tractor caps will be demanded as the price rises. Notice, however, that there is still an excess demand at $4.50. Therefore the same process will repeat itself for any price less than $5.

Suppose instead that the price were $6. Then we would have an excess amount of tractor caps sitting around. Producers would have offered more than people are willing to purchase at that price. In our example, producers would be offering 1000 tractor caps, but at $6 only 600 would be demanded, and producers would have an excess supply. Most of us have lived in a market-type economy long enough to know what will happen: a "sale." Some producers will offer their product for less by cutting the price. As the price falls, the quantity demanded will increase. Of course, fewer amounts of the good will be offered for sale. We will see tractor caps marked down to $5.50, then to $5, until the number of tractor caps produced over time is the same as the amount of tractor caps that people wish to purchase. At this point the market will be in equilibrium.

It seems logical to ask if markets are really ever in equilibrium. The answer to this question can be found by looking around you. Do you see a number of goods or services for which there is a large excess demand or excess supply? In economies that are based upon the market system, such as that of the United States, the answer is no. There may be certain times and certain products at certain places where there is excess demand or supply, but generally if you wish to purchase something at the market price, you can obtain it. When you get an instance like the gasoline lines of 1973, where people were waiting for hours to purchase gasoline, or could not purchase gasoline on certain days, it is a case where the price system has not been allowed to operate. In situations like this it is also likely that the market has not been allowed to operate because of some form of government intervention. When left to the free market, however, shortages are usually quickly eliminated through increases in price.

The same is true of excess supply of a good or service. We do not normally see unwanted inventories sitting around for lengthy periods of time. Sales, rebates, and markdowns take care of problems in the short run, and retailers then begin ordering less. Producers then have excess inventories and lower their prices to the retailer and begin producing less.

The same is true of labor services. If there is an excess of accounting services, we see salaries for accountants, especially starting accountants, going down relative to other salaries. This signals to existing accountants that they might reexamine their other opportunities, maybe becoming an attorney, a football coach, or whatever their next best opportunity is. Students will turn to professions other than accounting, as the opportunity cost of becoming something other than an accountant has now declined. Thus the market for accountants adjusts over time to eliminate the excess supply.

Applications

Having learned to put the basic tools of analysis together, the time has come to put them to use. There are three basic situations we will look at, but you will quickly notice that they encompass an infinite number of everyday circumstances. These three situations are a shift in the supply curve, a shift in the demand curve, and fixing the market price at something other than equilibrium.

Let us first observe a case of a shift in the supply curve. In August of 1990, Iraq invaded Kuwait, disrupting the potential supply of oil to world markets. This led to an increase in the price of oil from $20 per barrel to over $40 per barrel in a very short period. The question is, what do you think happened to the price and quantity of gasoline sold in the market? Well, the first thing to notice is that oil is used in the production of gasoline: it is an input. Recall that a rise in the price of an input will reduce the quantity supplied at every price and cause the supply curve to shift to the left. From this shift we notice a rise in price and that the quantity sold declines. This is shown in figure 4-2.

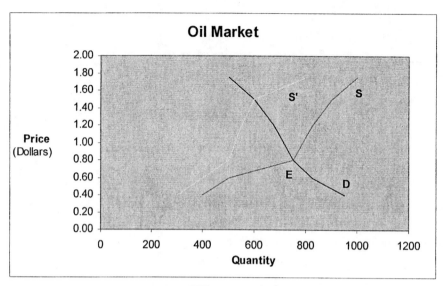

Figure 4-2

Let's further examine what has occurred. When analyzing this type of situation, we generally begin with the equilibrium conditions. This is logical because, as we mentioned above, in a market economy there usually is not a large excess supply or demand of a product. In our example, then, we begin at the point labeled E, where the price is at equilibrium, that is, where the original demand and supply curves, D and S, intersect. The equilibrium price is $0.80 per gallon and the equilibrium quantity is 750 gallons of gasoline. The rise in the price of oil shifts the supply curve to the left, to S'. Notice that the demand curve, D, has not shifted, as we did not allow for changes in people's tastes for gasoline, changes in income, or changes in the prices of substitutes or complements for gasoline.

With a new supply curve and the old demand curve, can the price remain for long at the old equilibrium price of $0.80? Look at how much gasoline would be supplied at $0.80. With the shift to S', the amount supplied would no longer be 750 gallons, but 500 gallons. The quantity demanded would remain at 750 gallons, however, so there would be excess demand for gasoline. We have already noticed that such a situation will not long remain in a freely operating market. As gasoline producers find that they run out of gasoline at the current price, the price will be raised and greater quantities will be supplied. Some customers will pay a higher price in order to make sure they have gasoline. Others, however, will no longer demand as much gasoline as they did at the lower price, and quantity demanded will decrease. The price and quantity supplied will continue to rise until the quantity demanded falls to the point where it is again equal to quantity supplied. This is at the price where the new supply curve, S', intersects the demand curve, D. At $1.50 the market will have again reached equilibrium, where quantity demanded equals quantity supplied, and the quantity sold in the market at this price

36

will be 600 gallons. The net result of the Iraqi invasion on the market for gasoline was an increase in the price of gasoline and a reduction in the amount of gasoline produced and sold.

Notice two things. First, if the price were not allowed to rise to $1.50, then the excess demand would remain in the market. Second, by the price rising to $1.50, there is a larger amount of gasoline produced than there would be if the price were to remain at $0.80.

For our second example of a shift in the supply curve we will begin with a question: what is the effect of an improvement in the technology of production on market price and quantity sold? When new products are introduced, isn't it usually the case that they are relatively expensive and that relatively few of them are sold? Think, for example, of television sets, video cassette recorders, cam corders, compact disc players, and other entertainment products. At first only a few of our wealthier friends have them. But we know that if we wait, the price will come down, and we will be able to get a piece of the action. Is there something magic about this? We now have a reasonable explanation for this phenomena. When these products are new, the technology of producing them is relatively primitive. But as the product is developed, the technology of producing them advances, and the production methods change. This basically means that producers are now willing to supply more VCRs, for example, at each price than they would before. We represent this as a shift in the supply curve to the right.

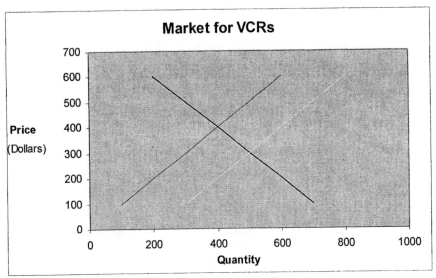

Figure 4-3

Imagine that Figure 4-3 shows the market for VCRs when they first become commercially available. The equilibrium price and quantity in the market are determined by the intersection of the demand and supply curves, D and S. The price and quantity we observe in the market will be $400 and 400 VCRs. But as the product matures (in these days at ever-faster rates) there is an improvement in the technology of production. Because of this the supply curve shifts to the right, from S to S'.

Now if the price remained at the old equilibrium price, $400, there would be an excess supply. Quantity supplied would be 600 VCRs, whereas quantity demanded would be 400 VCRs. Some suppliers would be willing to reduce their price and sell more of their product. The lowering of the price moves us down the demand curve as individuals buy more of the good and more individuals buy the good at lower prices. The new equilibrium will be at a lower price and a greater quantity sold in the market, $200 and 500 VCRs.

Let us now look at a shift in the demand curve. How can we explain the results of advertising? The purpose of advertising is to influence people's tastes for a product. Much advertising does not give you any information regarding the price of the product. Rather it attempts to get you to purchase more of the product than you otherwise would have at each price. Advertising tells us that if we drink a certain kind of beer we will have better looking girlfriends, or our parties will be more entertaining, and so on. We are not told that we should purchase more of this particular brand of beer because its price is going down. The advertiser is attempting to shift our demand so that we are willing to buy more at every given price. To the extent that advertisers are successful, our preferences will change and the market demand curve will shift to the right. This is shown in Figure 4-4.

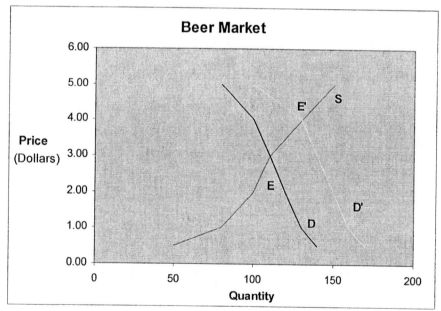

Figure 4-4

38

As usual, we begin with the market in equilibrium at the point E, with a price of $3 and a quantity of 110 six packs. The advertising campaign shifts the demand curve from D to D'. By now we can see that the new equilibrium will be at a higher price and a greater quantity of beer sold. Here the new demand curve, D', intersects the supply curve, S, at E'. The new price and quantity sold are $4 and 130 six-packs. Had the price not changed, there would be an excess demand for the beer, i.e., the quantity demanded at that price would be greater than the quantity supplied.

Let us look at another shift in the demand curve based not on a change in people's tastes, but rather on changes in prices of substitutes and complements. When we actually observe what is going on around us, namely that all manner of goods and services are at our disposal without us having to create them, it becomes clear that there is a great deal of interaction involved. One clear demonstration of this is the case of substitute and complementary goods.

Recall that we introduced these concepts earlier in our discussion of demand. Substitute goods are those for which the demand increases when the price of the other good rises, e.g., canned peaches and applesauce. The demand for complements goes down when the price of the other good rises, e.g., hot dogs and hot dog buns. Let us use this concept to show that an increase in the price of oil can result in a decrease in the price of beer, something that is not at first blush obvious to most of us.

Suppose the price of oil increases. We have already seen that oil is an input in the production of gasoline, and that an increase in the price of oil causes an increase in the price of gasoline. But gasoline is also an input into the good "pizza delivered to my house," as most pizzas are delivered by persons driving cars that run on gasoline. Thus the same reasoning we used before would lead us to predict a shift of the supply curve of home-delivered pizza to the left and an increase in the price of the good "pizza delivered to my house." Let us also suppose that pizzas are salty, and that there is nothing like an ice-cold beer to drink with my pizza. When a pizza is delivered to my house, I usually drink beer with it. This indicates that beer and home-delivered pizzas are complements. When the price of home-delivered pizza goes up, I am willing to buy less beer at every price of beer because I will buy fewer home-delivered pizzas. This means that the demand curve for beer has shifted to the left, as in Figure 4-5.

39

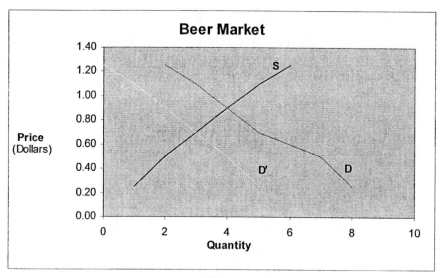

Figure 4-5

The original demand curve for beer is labeled D, and the supply curve is labeled S. The shift of the demand curve is indicated by the new demand curve, D', where fewer units of beer are purchased at every price. The original equilibrium price for beer is $0.90 per bottle. The new equilibrium price will be $0.70 per bottle. This illustrates what we originally set out to prove, that an increase in the price of oil will cause the price of beer to decrease. Note that the increase in oil prices has also caused the quantity of beer purchased to go down.

One can create a myriad of examples of shifts in the demand and supply curves and what the new equilibrium prices and quantities will be. The hard part is determining whether the supply curve or the demand curve has shifted—or if both have shifted—and in which direction. Usually common sense is a good guide. The important thing to remember is that a change in the price of a good never shifts either the supply curve or the demand curve for that good. For example, if the supply curve for CDs shifts to the left for some reason, it will cause the price of CDs to rise. However, this rise in the price of CDs can never shift the demand curve for CDs. The rise in the price of CDs occurs as you move up the demand curve for CDs with the shifting supply curve. The change in the price of CDs can shift the demand curve for substitutes for CDs, such as audio cassettes, but never the demand curve for the good itself.

The third and final situation to look at is one where the market does not reach equilibrium. The primary cause of this is usually some form of government intervention in the market. Examples include minimum wage legislation and rent control. Let us look at two possibilities, one in which the government fixes a minimum price above equilibrium, and one where government fixes a maximum price below equilibrium.

Minimum wage laws are good examples of government price fixing above equilibrium. Consider the labor market as a case where producers demand labor and workers sell it. The price for labor is usually called the wage. As with any other good, we would expect the quantity demanded of labor services to increase as the wage falls. Remembering that you cannot pay me more than the value of the added product I produce, you are more likely to want to hire me at $4 per hour than you would be at $400 per hour.

We also would expect the supply curve for labor to slope upward. People must be paid the value of their opportunity cost in order to get them to work. As the wage increases, it is more likely that it will exceed the opportunity cost of a person's time, and thus it is more likely that he or she will want to supply their labor. Increases in the wage, then, result in increases in the quantity of labor supplied. This is shown by the upward-sloping supply curve in figure 4-6.[12]

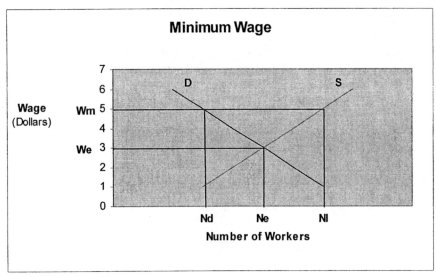

Figure 4-6

Suppose the equilibrium wage, where demand for labor equals the supply of labor, is at $3 per hour, as shown in figure 4-6 where D is the demand for labor and S is the supply (We is the equilibrium wage and Wm is the minimum wage). And suppose that the government determines that the minimum wage anyone can pay is $5 per hour. As we look at figure 4-6, we can see what will happen. The quantity of labor demanded will be less than was the case at $3 per hour, and the quantity of labor supplied will be greater than at $3 per hour. This results in what is known as unemployment. The number of persons looking for jobs minus the number of workers producers actually want (Nl minus Nd) is the amount of unemployment

---

[12] One can, using a higher level of economic theory, construct examples where the supply curve will bend backwards at some point. This is not of importance for our purposes here.

that will result. These are people who are actively seeking work and cannot find jobs. Thus, the first effect of the minimum wage is to cause unemployment.

Notice also that there are fewer jobs being provided. In equilibrium the amount of labor being used was Ne. If we assume that the government cannot force employers to hire people, then the amount of labor being used at $5 per hour is Nd. The people from Ne to Nd are laid off.

It will always be the case that if a price is set above equilibrium, the demand curve will determine the amount of a good or service that will be produced and consumed. This is because at a price higher than equilibrium, those demanding the service or good will always demand less than they would if the price were allowed to fall to equilibrium.

Next, let us look at the case where a maximum price is legislated. Suppose that the government will not allow me to rent my apartment at more than $400 per month. And suppose that the equilibrium price for rental housing is $500 per month, as shown in Figure 4-7, where D is the demand for rental housing and S is the supply of rental housing. At $400 per month the quantity supplied of rental housing will be Qs, and the quantity demanded of rental housing will be Qd. Obviously, the quantity demanded is greater than the quantity supplied (Qd minus Qs). This is called a shortage (the difference between quantity demanded and quantity supplied at the going price). In the absence of government regulation, this shortage would be eliminated by the market, since the price would rise and we would move up the supply curve and down the demand curve until we reached equilibrium. Thus, rent control will produce a shortage of rental housing.

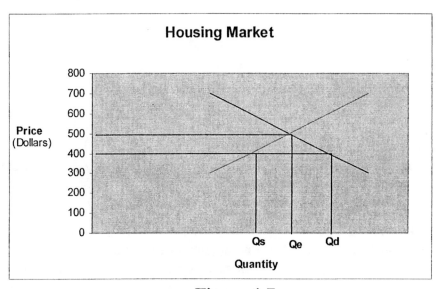

Figure 4-7

We should notice that, again, the output that will exist in the market will be less than would have existed at equilibrium. In this case, it is because the government cannot force suppliers to bring to market the amount necessary to meet the demand. Whenever the government does not allow the market price to move to equilibrium there will be less output than would be the case without government intervention.

Let us look at a final example that will combine some of the elements of demand and supply as well as explicitly take into account the interrelationships of markets.

Suppose the federal government decides to declare a war on the illicit drug industry. Suppose also that the way it will wage this war is to reduce the supply of marijuana by destroying marijuana crops and arresting sellers of marijuana. These actions will shift the supply curve of marijuana to the left causing a rise in the equilibrium price and a decrease in the quantity of marijuana produced and consumed. But notice if the demand for marijuana is inelastic in the relevant range, then the percentage decrease in quantity consumed will be smaller than the percentage increase in the price, and thus total spending on marijuana will increase.

Also notice that the increase in the price of marijuana will result in a shift to the right of the demand for substitutes for marijuana, such as cocaine. This will lead to an increase in the price of cocaine and an increase in the quantity produced and consumed of cocaine. It will also result in an increase in the amount spent on cocaine, since both price and quantity of cocaine are rising.

The interested reader can examine the effects of an alternative strategy, such as shifting the demand curve for marijuana to the left by altering preferences through advertising, or by arresting consumers of marijuana.

Summary

Since we have covered quite a bit of material in this chapter, a summary of some key ideas may be helpful. First, by putting the demand and supply curves together we can establish the equilibrium price and quantity that will prevail in a market. Any price lower than this will result in more of the good being demanded than will be supplied, a shortage. Any price higher than this will result in more of the good being supplied than is demanded, excess supply. In either case the incentives are to move to equilibrium.

Shifts in either the demand curve or the supply curve will create an initial state of shortage or of excess supply. The price will then change, establishing a new equilibrium price and quantity. The key to this analysis is recognizing which of the two curves, demand or supply, has shifted.

Finally, government may attempt to fix a price at something other than equilibrium. This will result in either a shortage or an excess of supply. This must also create a situation where less of the good is produced in the market than if the price had been left to move to equilibrium.

And now on to chapter 5 and a discussion of the role of profit.

Chapter 5

PROFIT

The ability to earn profit is one of the most important aspects of a market economy. Profit not only rewards individuals for taking risks and pleasing consumers, but it also acts as a market signal in the same way prices do. Eliminate profit, and the flow of resources to their most valued use and the efficient management of resources will be damaged. Let's take a closer look.

Economic Profit

Profit is usually defined as total revenue minus total cost. This is what we may call accounting profit. Economic profit, on the other hand, is the return the owner of a resource receives which is greater than the opportunity cost of that resource. In order to earn economic profit, the owner of a firm must earn at least as much from the use of the resources as he would earn using those resources in another industry. A firm, then, is making economic profit when it is earning "above normal" profit.

Let us look at a simple example. Suppose you own what is called a "party store" in the Midwest, a "package store" in the East, or a "liquor store" in the West. Suppose at the end of the year that your accountant finds your sales were $100,000, and that the payments to all the owners of resources, such as your workers, the owner of your building, your suppliers, etc. are $80,000. She then notifies you that you earned a profit of $20,000. But at this point an economist would be unable to say that you had earned economic profit. It depends upon whether or not you worked at the store and the opportunity cost of your time, for one thing. If you worked at the store and could have instead made $22,000 peeling potatoes at the local Burger King, then you would have to consider this as part of your costs: you would have made a loss of $2,000. Or suppose you could have used those same resources in running a video rental store and made $25,000. Your talents as a video store owner would have been greater than your talents as a party store owner, and thus after adding in your opportunity cost, you would have earned no economic profit.

Effect on Supply

Now let's think for a moment about what happens when a firm produces a product and earns economic profit. This means it is earning more from the use of its resources than those resources could earn somewhere else. Other entrepreneurs will notice that this firm is in an industry that earns more than they are earning in their industry. Some of them will choose to enter the industry where this extra profit can be made. But we already know what happens as additional firms enter the industry from our analysis of supply in Chapter 3. The new firms entering will shift the supply curve for the product to the right, as in figure 5-1.

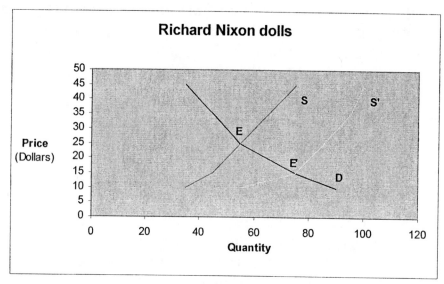

Figure 5-1

Let figure 5-1 represent the market for Richard Nixon dolls. The original equilibrium is at E, where the market price is $25 with 55 dolls per week being produced. Now suppose at this price that firms producing Richard Nixon dolls are making a 12% rate of return on their resources, and that the normal rate of return is 8%. Some firms will notice this and begin producing the dolls, shifting the supply curve to the right and causing equilibrium to move to E'. At this point the price has fallen to $15, and the output is 75 dolls per week.

The profits made in this industry encouraged new entrants. Shifting the supply curve to the right drove the price of the product down and increased the output of the product. More resources have gone into this industry, and some of those resources have left other industries. New entrants will follow until the price has fallen enough to eliminate the economic profit. The market system will have directed resources into their most highly valued use since resources will enter the industry until economic profit goes to zero, or until resources cannot earn more than they do anywhere else.

Profits Tax

Now what would have happened had we taxed away these profits? Well, for one, there would be no incentive for other firms to enter the industry, pushing down prices and increasing the amount of product available. As a group, consumers would be worse off because resources would continue to be used where they are less valued. But there is another problem with taxing away profits, and that is its effect on the incentive to innovate.

Notice that earning profit in a market system is a temporary phenomenon. Recall that we are talking about economic profit and not accounting profit. If a firm does not earn enough accounting profit to pay the opportunity cost of the resources used in the production of its good or service, then that firm will eventually go out of business. Thus, we would expect to see firms earn accounting profit over time. General Motors, since it uses a vast amount of resources, must earn the opportunity cost of that vast amount of resources every year, and so we would expect it to have enormous accounting profit over time. But we would not expect it to have economic profit in the sense that it earns more with its resources in the production of automobiles than those resources can earn in the production of something else. If it did, other firms would enter the automobile production industry, driving down the price of automobiles and increasing output until all the existing firms earned no economic profit.

People and firms can earn temporary economic profits only by making above-average use of one's resources. This often means inventing a less expensive way to produce, that is, improving the production technology. If you are producing hats, and you invent a way of producing hats that reduces the labor cost by 20%, then you will be able to sell your hats at the same price as your competitors, but your costs will be lower, and thus you will earn economic profit. Eventually your competitors will find it useful to adopt your method of production, or an even better one. When they do, the supply curve for the product will shift to the right (recall the effect of an advance in production technology on the supply curve from Chapter 3), thus driving down the price of hats and increasing the number of hats sold. Eventually your economic profit will disappear as you are forced to lower the price of your hats to meet the challenge of your competitors. However, it will take some time for this to occur, and you will have earned economic profit in the meantime. If you continue to advance the technology, then you can continue to earn economic profit until your competitors catch up. The reward for innovating may be enormous. The lure of being able to drive a Rolls Royce or donate millions to a favorite charity will drive people to find ways to get more output from the same amount of resources. This is conservation at its best.

Suppose you were not able to keep the profits you earned from your advancement of production technology. What incentive would you have to improve the production system? Very little, and that was one of the problems with the planned economies of Eastern Europe. They ended up producing shoddy products at enormous resource cost. The environmental resources of these countries were used up at a frightening pace because there was no incentive to learn to use them better. No one was able to keep the profit they might earn from discovering how to produce more cheaply.

Think about inventing new products. When you are the first to arrive on the market with a successful product, you have no competitors. In this period you may be able to earn enormous profit. Every Christmas some toy manufacturer is blessed with this situation. Play Station Games and Beanie Babies are well-known examples, but every year it is something different. Why are we in the market economy always bombarded with new and exciting (or even silly) products? Because the first one to come to market with a new product can make profits. Now, of course, the same story that we have already laid out will unfold. Imitators of these new products will soon come to market if they see economic profit being made. Soon the price will begin to fall as these new firms enter, and the output will increase. Two months after Christmas there will be ten different dolls that closely resemble Beanie Babies, and their prices will be lower, as will the price of the originals.

And again we ask what if the profits are taxed away? Then there is no incentive to invent any new product. There is no signal to entrepreneurs to buy resources and enter an industry. And all of this ends up in a stagnated economy. Eastern Europe once more provides a striking example. Not only were their products shabby and resources used inefficiently, but they had vastly fewer and very outdated products. The merging of East and West Germany must have been like stepping into consumer heaven from the perspective of the East Germans, who had been subject to a planned economy for many, many years.

The Producer's Budget Constraint

In a market economy the only budget constraint on a producer is the revenues received from product sales. You might ask, what if I invent the better mousetrap that would have the world beating a path to my door, but am poor and don't have the financing to produce and market it? Doesn't that mean that I cannot participate in the market economy and its rewards for being inventive? It does not, because you have the ability to earn profit. You may not have a dime in your pocket, but if you can convince someone or a group of persons that you have a good idea that will be purchased by consumers, then they will lend the money to you to start your business. Why would they be willing to lend you money? Because the market rewards risk. If you convince me you have a good idea, then I will lend you the money because I stand to make money for taking the risk that your idea might fail and that you might not be able to pay me back. I may become a partner, either active or silent, rather than loan you the money. Still, I am financing your idea in order to earn a return for myself. And again, if the profit you might earn is taxed away, then there is no incentive for me to take the risk of financing your idea. When there is reward for risk taking, then anyone with an idea can seek out financing to make the idea into a marketable product. When profits are taxed away, then no one will be able to get financial assistance.

Those who want to impose heavy taxes on profits are suffering from the same problem as those who think that they can reduce murders by mandating capital punishment for people carrying a firearm while selling illegal drugs: they are not looking at the true effects on people's behavior. By taxing away firms' profits we are not merely taking away assets from the wealthy, but also are subjecting every person in the economy to higher prices, fewer goods, and misuse of our precious resources. A tax on profit will have effects that will make us all poorer in the long run.

Chapter 6

┌───┐
└───┘

THE MARKET ECONOMY VS.
A PLANNED ECONOMY

Ludwig von Mises, the well-known economist, wrote prolifically and with great clarity about the advantages of a market economy over an economy with state allocation of resources. Indeed, in 1922 he demonstrated that socialism[13] cannot survive as an economic system.[14] This became clear to the world with the fall of the Iron Curtain in 1989, exposing an economic system which had been unable to provide a decent standard of living for people, and which left the environment in shambles. Mises had been correct.

The discussion in this chapter is based upon the insights and writings of Professor von Mises.[15] I trust that paraphrasing him will make his points clear and hope that this chapter will entice the reader to seek out a few of his classic works.

There are three basic points to grasp from the following discussion. First, Professor von Mises established that a market economy allocates resources efficiently. Then, by showing that consumers ultimately determine wages, he made the point that the distribution of income is generally fair in a market economy. Finally, he showed that the market economy is the only method of organizing society to allocate resources that is consistent with individual liberty.

Efficiency of Resource Use

As pointed out in earlier chapters, price signals and the profit motive in a market economy act to provide information quickly and concisely so that resources are allocated to their most efficient use. When prices for a good are rising, this signals to producers that they should produce more of it; the profit motive encourages producers to make more of the good and other firms to enter the industry. When the price of a resource rises, this is a signal for producers to conserve on its use, to seek greater supplies of it, and to use less costly alternatives. Resources are conserved and put to uses most favored by consumers.

In a planned economy, none of this is possible. A planner can never know the vast amount of information needed to manage economic production. Just think of the difficulties that you would encounter if you were commissioned by the

---

[13] A system in which the state controls the allocation of resources.

[14] See *Socialism*, (1922; Indianapolis: Liberty Fund, 1981)

[15] For a discussion of his most famous works, see Murray Rothbard. "The Essential Mises," in Ludwig von Mises, *Planning for Freedom*, fourth edition (South Holland, Illinois: Libertarian Press, 1980).

government to oversee the pencil industry.[16] How could you ever garner enough information to know how many pencils to build, where to produce them, where to distribute them, as well as the exact mix of resources that minimizes the cost of producing them? This might be possible if the economy were stagnant so that once you had the answers you could simply let everything roll along. But we do not normally wish our economy to be stagnant. We hope that our economy is growing. But this means that the answers to the planner's questions will change every day, perhaps every hour. As you can see, planned economies will be swamped by the problems of too much or too little information, as well as a limited capability to process it.

Nobel laureate Friedrich Hayek, in a famous paper written more than half a century ago, pointed out that knowledge always exists in dispersed pieces possessed by separate individuals.[17] The economic problem, then, is how to make the best use of resources when people's wants, skills, and information cannot be known by any single person. This means that an economic system cannot expect to function properly when consciously controlled by a single individual or entity, but instead, the system must induce individuals to do desirable things without anyone having to tell them what to do. Of course, the market system based on prices and profit accomplishes exactly this.

To put this into perspective, imagine a controlled economic system anticipating a Beanie Baby craze, let alone coming up with such a doll in the first place. Or how about the success of the mini-van, first produced in the 1980's? Would a controlled economy ever have produced such a thing, or have been able to handle the huge demand for such a seemingly simple and logical innovation? What individual or entity could ever have anticipated such demands—and provided for them? Only a market system with innovation and profit-motivated individuals can produce such things.

There are, of course, lots of things we may not like about how the market allocates resources. For example, if you can't find a way to produce something that consumers want to buy, then you will be very poor. Those people who are unskilled, although they work very hard, may not produce anything of much value to consumers, and thus will live at a low standard of living. We may not like what the market produces with regards to disbursement of income. Like it or not, consumers may value entertainment more than culture, and thus boxers may make millions of dollars while poets make very little.

In a market economy, the distribution of income also depends upon initial distributions of resources—including educational resources—as well as luck and

---

[16] See Leonard Read's, "I Pencil, My Family Tree as Told to Leonard Read," in *The Freeman*, Foundation for Economic Education, December, 1958.

[17] See Friedrich Hayek, "The Us of Knowledge in Society," *American Economic Review*, XXXV, No. 4 (September, 1945), pp. 519-530.

effort. Even so, what the reasoning of Ludwig von Mises showed in the 1920's—and what the experience of this century has made abundantly clear—is that market economies will always vastly outperform planned economies. The result is that even the poorest of those in a market economy will be better off than most of those in a planned economy, and the total amount of goods and services available will be much greater when markets determine where resources are to be used.

Markets as a Fair System of Resource Allocation

Opposition to the market process often comes from two beliefs. The first is that the producers, or business owners, control the system and dictate outcomes to the consumers and laborers. The second is that markets are solely cutthroat systems where the object is to destroy the wealth of others.

As Mises often points out, in a market economy, consumers are king. There is really no such thing as a production tsar who can mandate how much of a good is to be produced and consumed. This is because in a true market economy no one can force you to purchase his product, and others are free to produce any good or service to compete with anyone else's good or service.

As an example, suppose I am the owner of a large integrated computer business involved in purchasing inputs, hiring labor, producing the computers and selling them at retail. I actually have very little control over what I pay my workers, purchase my inputs for, or the price at which I sell my computers. Of course, I could decide to charge $4000 for a low-power personal computer. But I cannot force anyone to buy my product. If my competitors are selling a similar computer for $1000, then no one will buy mine, and I will go out of business. The same holds true for how much I pay for my inputs. The price I must pay for microchips is whatever price is necessary to bid them away from others who wish to use the same microchips. I cannot dictate to my suppliers what I will pay. Offering too low a price will result in no one selling me microchips. This is also true of the labor I hire. I cannot dictate that I will pay $5 per hour for labor. If $5 an hour is not enough to meet a person's opportunity cost—what they could earn somewhere else—I will not obtain any labor. I also cannot pay my labor any more than the value of what they produce. Attempting to do so would leave me with a bankrupt business.

In a market economy it is the consumers that determine the price of products and resources and the incomes of owners of resources, including labor. As Mises put it, consumers ultimately pay the wages of all individuals. What this means is that a person's income ultimately depends on how well she satisfies consumer desires. If you are very good at satisfying consumer wants, such as Michael Jordan or Bill Gates, then you will be very wealthy. If you cannot satisfy consumer wants, (suppose you are a lyrical poet that cannot seem to sell any books of poetry), then you will be poor. In a market system, those who are wealthy may not work as hard as some others, they may not be as smart, they may not be as gifted, but they certainly produce something consumers are willing to pay for.

Even those who are born into wealth must at a minimum place their assets in something that produces a product that consumers desire. History is littered with those who went from extreme wealth to modest wealth or even poverty through "bad investments." Bad investment simply means that the person's resources were put into a scheme that did not produce something consumers were willing to purchase at a price greater than the alternative value of those resources.

Nor should we believe that the market system is a fierce one of survival at the expense of one's rivals. It is not what economists would call a zero-sum game, where what one person wins another person must lose. In fact, markets are very cooperative systems. Simply looking about you should make this clear. Just think how much you rely on others in your everyday activity. You expect that someone will produce your food, deliver your water, produce fuel, clothing, shelter, entertainment, and the myriad of the things that you consume in your daily life. A market economy is not one of isolated entrepreneurs each attacking one another. All producers rely on other producers for inputs, delivery systems, and all other facets of the production process, as well as relying on their employees to provide the labor necessary to produce a finished product. As Adam Smith points out, the development of the market system allowed specialization of labor which resulted in greater output than could have been imagined under any other system. But this specialization of labor is only possible in a system based upon cooperation.

Individual Freedom and Markets

There are many ways to define freedom. The Austrian school of economic analysis has as good a way as any when it describes freedom as a state where an individual is in a position to choose between alternative modes of action. This does not mean that you have the power to choose from all possible options, but simply that you are not bound to follow the mandates of another individual.

Mises points out that freedom is not constrained by the laws that are necessary to maintain the structure of a cooperative society. One cannot reap the benefits of a market society and at the same time be unconstrained from actions that would destroy the market system. As an example, a law against theft does not limit my freedom. This is because well-defined property rights are essential to market cooperation. If you are free to deprive me the fruits of my labor or to take away the benefits from my risking my assets in a new venture, then I will have much less incentive to work or to invest in new methods of production. Markets simply could not work in such an atmosphere. Thus, laws against theft actually increase my range of choice rather than reduce it, as the market system offers the greatest number of options to individuals.

There is really no kind of freedom other than the kind a market system provides. Economies where resources are not owned by individuals and goods and services, including labor services, are not freely exchanged, are unlikely to be free. Resources will be allocated in some fashion in any economy. If they are not allocated though free exchange, then the government will allocate them. But this power to allocate resources will naturally lead to diminution of all personal freedom.

Those who would argue that government-planned economies, such as socialist economies, retain non-economic freedoms, miss the point that there really is no distinction between economic freedom and non-economic freedoms. For example, take freedom of the press. If the government controls who receives paper, ink, and printing presses, there will be little freedom of the press. What we see today is a technological revolution that has broken down the ability of governments to control access to the resources necessary to produce information and opinion. It was this revolution that pushed along the perestroika of the Soviet Union. A market economy marked by free exchange and access to resources guarantees a free press.

As another example, what is the value of a trial by jury if the government has the ability to determine where I am to work? If I am charged with a crime and acquitted, the government could still send me to Siberia to work at subsistence wages in a coal mine.

The elimination of barriers to competition preserves freedom in a market-based economy. I have a choice of whom to work for and for how much as long as there is more than one employer in the economy. In a planned economy, the government is the only employer, and thus my freedom is eliminated. I am free to choose products as long as there is more than one product and there is no barrier to entering into competition with current producers. As Yale Brozen has pointed out, nearly all of the barriers to entry are the result of government regulation and other intervention.[18]

Technology acts to reduce barriers to entry. This is to be expected in a market economy because profit is made by entrepreneurs who are the first to produce a popular product. Efficient production while there is little competition creates profit. But this very profit encourages folks to invent ways of entering the market. Any industry where there are enormous profits is also an industry where there are enormous incentives to find a way to enter into production in that industry. Thus, despite, the observation of Adam Smith, that "People of the same

---

[18] See Yale Bozen, *Is Government the Source of Monopoly? and Other Essays* (Washington, D.C.: Cato Institute, 1981).

trade seldom meet together, even for merriment and diversion, but the conversation ends in a conspiracy against the public, or in some contrivance to raise prices,"[19] a market economy will naturally eliminate monopolies over time. Indeed, the larger the profits that exist from a monopoly the more sure one can be that the monopoly will be done in by new competitors. Choice and personal freedom are natural outcomes of market allocation of resources.

---

[19] Adam Smith, *Wealth of Nations*, Cannan ed., Methuen, 1904, vol. 1, p 130.

Chapter 7

THE LAW

More than one hundred and forty years ago, Frederic Bastiat wrote a book entitled *The Law*, in which he sets forth a proposition that gives us a slightly different way of thinking about our political system.[20] Bastiat's proposition is that all government stems from the individual's natural right to self-defense. Governments are the collective organization of individuals to defend their persons, their liberty, and their property. He also points out that preservation of any one of the three items, life, liberty, and property, depends upon the preservation of the other two.

Adopting Bastiat's viewpoint, let us ask a question: if governments and the laws they create and enforce are supposed to defend people and their private property, can it be just for a government to create a law that would destroy a person's right to life, liberty, and property? In particular, if law is the organization of individuals to defend themselves, can the law be used to seize an individual's property and distribute it to someone else?

Bastiat asks us to adopt a moral philosophy, to establish in our own minds what government may or may not do to preserve justice. Is there really any difference between my taking your property without your consent by outright robbing you and my taking your property by putting together a group in our community and passing a law that takes away your property? If there is, then we need to decide how to distinguish between the two cases, as well as what are the repercussions of adopting laws that enable us to take from one another.

Let us think of a simple example. Suppose you and I produce automobiles. Suppose also that you produce an automobile that consumers like better than mine. In a freely operating market, my response will have to be to lower the price of my automobiles, to improve the quality of my automobiles, or both. If I were to take $2000 from every person that walked into your showroom and bought a car, you would probably think this was not a just thing to do and that it should be against the law. But suppose instead that I hire a lobbyist who persuades Congress to pass a law that imposes a tax of $2000 on every car you sell because your cars are made somewhere else (a tariff), or use too much fuel (an energy saving tax), or are too expensive (a luxury tax). The result is exactly the same. Indeed, if you were to examine the myriad of taxes and regulations passed by your state and federal government, you would find that many of them, if not most, are simply taking from one person and giving to another, or giving one producer an advantage over another. The excuses used to justify these laws are quite ingenious. But stripped of

---

[20] *The Law* (1850, Irvington-on-Hudson: Foundation for Economic Education, 1981).

57

their slick rhetoric, they come down to what would be recognized as theft or plunder if done by an individual.

Bastiat points out that there are a number of inevitable results once people allow their government to engage in the practice of taking from one person and giving to another. The first is that it becomes very important who makes the laws. It also will be important to be able to influence those persons to make laws favorable to you or unfavorable your competitors.

Of course, we are now reaping what has been sown. In California it costs more than $40 million to run for the United States Senate. How can it be that a person is willing to raise $40 million to run for a Senate job that pays less than $200 thousand per year? Because the Senate seat brings with it enormous power—the power to seize and redistribute untold billions of dollars of wealth. And why should people be willing to spend thousands of dollars entertaining Senators and taking them on trips to the Caribbean? Because that Senator can ruin your business with the passage of a single law—or ruin your competitor's business with the passage of another.

Corruption in government, expensive lobbying, multi-million-dollar campaigns, a Congress and state legislature made up of lifetime politicians, and all the problems of government that are obvious to everyone will continue to exist because we have accepted the premise that it is a proper role of government (and that it is morally just) to take from those who are in the minority to give to those who can influence the majority of our representatives. To put it bluntly, we deserve the government we get.

To think that it is possible for Congress to pass a campaign spending law that will not favor incumbents and that cannot be circumvented by a very expensive lawyer is to whistle in the dark. The rewards from influencing government are enormous, and the larger the government's role, the larger those rewards. It is impossible to have such incentives in our system and not have them produce the problems we see every day.

Consonant with this reality, Bastiat suggested in 1850 that it is not the legislator who is at fault, but rather the system. Scandals therefore will continue and will get larger as government's role in influencing outcomes and taking property expands, no matter who the legislators, congressmen, or bureaucrats are. When the Environmental Protection Agency can shut down my plant which produces $450 million worth of product every year, don't you think I will hire a lobbyist to make sure that those who make such decisions at the EPA know what a good thing it is for my plant to be operating? If you pass a law that says I can't take a bureaucrat to lunch, won't I invite him over to my house for dinner?

Reflect upon these words of Bastiat and how relevant they are to today's political environment, although written in another century on another continent:

As long as it is admitted that the law may be diverted from its true purpose—

that it may violate property instead of protecting it—then everyone will want to participate in making the law, either to protect himself against plunder or to use it for plunder. Political questions will always be prejudicial, dominant, and all-absorbing.[21]

Today, there is a sub-discipline of the economics profession called the theory of rent-seeking which confirms the fact that what Bastiat says is true. Economists call the practice of spending resources to influence the outcome of government in order to better one's position "rent-seeking." Articles by the dozen attempt to explain why rent-seeking occurs, estimate the loss in resources that occurs because of rent-seeking, the optimum method of rent-seeking, etc. But the bottom line is that as long as the government is able to create laws that subvert our rights to property, then rent-seeking will occur.

A second effect of accepting government's ability to take from one person and give to another as just is the erasing of the line distinguishing justice from injustice. When you think it is morally right for the government to pass a law that takes my property from me and gives it to you, then you must either give up your moral sense or your respect for the law. For how can you distinguish between robbery by a gang of thieves and those taking your grandmother's property through a property tax?

Bastiat labels the situation where government power is used in violation of the maxim that government is organized to protect an individual's right to property "legalized plunder." He gives us a prescription for identifying legalized plunder: (1) see if the law takes from some persons that which belongs to them and gives it to another person to whom it does not belong, and (2) see if the law benefits one person or persons at the expense of another by doing what the other person could not do without committing a crime.[22]

Let's look at a couple of examples. In 1989, San Francisco, California sustained a severe earthquake. Millions of dollars worth of damage was done, and several persons were killed. The California legislature responded by passing an increase in the state sales tax with the revenue from the additional tax going to aid the persons who suffered in the earthquake.

Now, at first you might say that this is a just and compassionate law. How nice of the people of the rest of California to aid those unfortunate enough to have been caught in an earthquake. But let us now look at the situation from Bastiat's perspective.

What does this law actually do? It takes the property of my parents who live in Fresno, California by requiring them to give up some of their income every time they purchase a taxable item. Their property is then given to someone they don't

---

[21] *Ibid.*, p 18.
[22] Ibid., p. 21.

know in the San Francisco Bay area. The person receiving the money that the state provides could not have directly taken my mother's money to fix up their house, but the government is free to take my mother's money and give it to that same person for repairs.

You might say, but shouldn't we take care of the less fortunate? Doesn't the government have an obligation to do something for the victims? The answer to the first question is "yes." But the answer to the second is "not necessarily." What Bastiat points out is that being against the government taking its citizens property to do something does not mean a person is against the activity the government would be undertaking. In our example, most of us would probably say that we should help the victims. But we should either do this as individuals or as voluntarily organized groups of individuals.

Politicians who wish to take the property of others to affect some outcome will often argue that if you are against the government action you are against the outcome. If you argue against the government levying taxes to provide education you are therefore against education. This is an attempt to deflect the debate away from what is the proper role of government to whether certain outcomes would be nice to have. One way of thinking about this is to ask if a politician should be able to use your money to contribute to his or her favorite charity. The answer, if one accepts Bastiat's concept of justice, is no.

Bastiat goes on to point out that much of what the government does is false philanthropy. The California sales tax for earthquake victims is a case-in-point. It is not a true philanthropic action, whereby people freely give of their own time, talent and treasure to assist others. In fact, the government offers a sad commentary on the condition of mankind in that it does not feel that people will assist their fellow men and women unless their property is taken by force.

Herbert Spencer, writing in England at about the same time Bastiat writes in France, notes that there is what might be called a lessening of our morality as a society when people rely on the government to provide assistance.[23] It is not so much that those receiving the assistance become dependent on it, but that as individuals we begin to ignore those of us who are less fortunate than we are. Rather than giving of ourselves to take care of the poor, our reaction is to say that the government takes a large fraction of our income, and therefore it is the government's responsibility to take care of them.

Bastiat broadens this concept to say that the more government undertakes and attempts to justify its expansion in our lives, the more likely it is for people to blame the government as things go wrong. People even begin to blame the government for problems the government has no power or right to influence.

---

[23] Herbert Spencer's "The Proper Sphere of Government" was published in 1842. It is included in *The Man Versus the State* (Indianapolis: Liberty Fund, 1982).

60

The primary problem with using philanthropy as a measure of what government should be engaged in is that unlike justice, philanthropy has no limit. If you take the position that just laws are those that protect life, liberty, and property, and unjust laws are those which violate these rights, then the area of debate on whether something is the proper role of government is made considerably smaller. One could argue that public education is the proper role of government under the theory that the rights of children to purchase as much education as they wish needs to be protected, since their parents could conceivably choose to purchase no education for them. Then the children would grow up unskilled, and their wages over their lifetime would be much smaller than they would be otherwise. Bastiat would not agree with this conclusion, but that is the way in which the argument must be framed. While there is much that government might be engaged in that could be argued is for the protection of life, liberty, and property, the bulk of what government does would be seen as unjust. There would be limits to what government can do.

If, on the other hand, government is able to do whatever is philanthropic from its point of view, then there is theoretically no limit to government's role. Let us go back to the earthquake example. Is there any reasonable difference between persons who built their homes on a fault line in California and then suffered damage in an earthquake and those who built their homes in a flood plain and suffered damage from a flood? Of course not. Well, what about those who suffer damage from hurricanes? Or those that suffer damage from droughts?

It then becomes clear that under the philanthropic view, government's role is quite broad indeed. It may take my income and property to give to anyone who suffers from a natural disaster.

I live in Hillsdale, Michigan. The roads in Hillsdale County often become very slippery with snow in the winter (and spring, unfortunately). Suppose I am driving back from doing some consulting work in Lansing, and as I near Hillsdale my car spins out on an icy road and hits a tree. Now is that any different than the person who built their home on a flood plain and suffers flood damage? I can certainly make an argument that the government should take your money and give it to me to fix my car if it can take my money to fix your house.

The hard fact is that government cannot create wealth, but can only seize and redistribute it. In order to provide a grant to an artist to finish a painting it must take someone else's property. To provide education to children it must take someone's income to build the school and pay the teachers. While we may decide that there are some things government should do, we should examine each governmental proposal with the fact in mind that anything government gives to one person must be taken from another.

Chapter 8

INDIVIDUAL LIBERTY

Friedrich Hayek, the 1974 Nobel Laureate in economics, begins his 1960 book, *The Constitution of Liberty*, by alerting us of the need to clarify our aims and principles.[24] This is even more important some forty years later as Eastern Europe, Africa, Latin America, and other places struggle to establish new economic and political orders. What should these peoples, as well as our own, use as a guideline to organize their social and economic orders?

This nation was founded on the guiding principle that individual liberty is to be cherished. But what do we mean by individual liberty, and why should we care about it? And if we do believe that individual liberty is the foundation for societal order, how do we go about making it so?

Liberty: What It Is and What It Isn't

Let us begin by trying to define liberty. Hayek defines it as the possibility of a person acting according to his or her own decision and plan. Liberty is not necessarily having an unlimited number of courses of action open to you. Rather, it is the state of being where a person has a set of opportunities for action with which no one can interfere.

What this means is that you are free, or have individual liberty, when, given your circumstances, no one can coerce you into making a choice you would rather not make. As an example, suppose you are very poor, have grown up in poverty in rural Indiana, have barely completed high school, and are working at the local gas station. I, on the other hand, am the son of a billionaire baseball player and have just graduated from the finest undergraduate college in the country. You may not be able to choose to enroll at Yale Law School next year because your background and circumstances make it impossible for you to achieve that goal. I, on the other hand, can choose to go to Yale to start my brilliant law career.

In Hayek's view, we are both free as long as no one can interfere with our decisions about what to do next. Remember, freedom is not defined as having the widest range of possible choices. Your freedom lies in the fact that no one can tell you that you cannot choose to attend the local community college and work towards your goal. My freedom is similar in that no one can tell me that I cannot apply to Yale because blue-eyed persons are not allowed to become lawyers.

---

[24] (Chicago: University of Chicago Press, 1960). Much of the discussion in this and the following two chapters is owed to Professor Hayek's work.

63

By this definition then, liberty lies in lack of coercion rather than numbers of options. Wealthy people or people with certain backgrounds may seem to have a wider range of feasible options, but that doesn't mean they are more free. You still have liberty even though you are constrained by a particular set of circumstances. This is very different from being constrained by another individual having power to veto your choice and substitute his or her will for your own.

Oftentimes liberty or freedom is confused with power. Bastiat makes the point in *The Law* that liberty is not the same as power. He uses the example of education. The power to receive an education can be given by the state, but from whom does the state obtain the power to give an education? The only way the state can provide you with an education is to take the resources away from other uses. This can only be accomplished by taking from someone else.

Hayek writes about the confusion people like John Dewey and John R. Commons create when they argue that liberty is a freedom from obstacles. If you define liberty as freedom from obstacles, then things quickly become confusing, and the definition comes very close to arguing that liberty is wealth: the more wealth you have the more types of obstacles you can overcome, and thus the more liberty you possess. This leads to the conclusion that you can increase liberty by taking from the wealthy and distributing this wealth among the less wealthy. But this is really saying that persons can be coerced into doing things they otherwise wouldn't do, i.e., to give up their property to those who wish to redistribute it.[25] Can a definition of liberty that leads to such conclusions be correct?

In the past, liberty had been established in certain places through the granting of particular liberties. The Magna Charta, for example (written in the thirteenth century), established some bounds for the power of the King of England and set forth certain things that individuals could do without interference from the King. However, there is a tremendous difference between prohibiting all actions unless they are specifically allowed, and allowing all actions unless they are specifically prohibited. Life in the United States is based upon the latter concept; that is, you are free to act unless a law specifically prohibits your action. This is consonant with the notion that liberty is freedom from coercion.

This idea was nothing new to the Greeks of years ago. According to Hayek, free persons (not all persons were free) in ancient Greece had five basic rights which defined their freedom. These were: 1) the legal status of a protected member of society, 2) freedom from arbitrary arrest, 3) the right to do whatever the individual desires unless specifically prohibited, 4) the right to free movement, and 5) the right to own property. This is not a bad list of rights to describe freedom in

---

[25] Of course, we have already seen that Bastiat would consider such a situation unjust since the government would be doing exactly the opposite of protecting life, liberty, and property.

any society. Possession of such basic rights protects a person's freedom and defends one against coercion.

Why Liberty is Important

Having established a definition of freedom, let's be more specific about what we mean by coercion. Hayek's definition is a useful one. Coercion is when you are forced to act, not according to your own plan, but to serve the ends of another. Now the question remains, why is it important that people be free from coercion? One obvious answer is to satisfy the notion that individual freedom is important for its own sake. But an equally important reason, the implications of which are not as immediately obvious, is that coercion eliminates the importance of the individual as a thinking and valuable person.

Hayek is very concerned about the use of knowledge in society. In an earlier chapter we discussed one wonder of the market process is that it allows production and distribution to occur without requiring the vast amounts of information that encumber a command economy. How is this so? Through the knowledge and talent of freely acting individuals. Individual persons respond to incentives and make decisions based upon prices and profit, resulting in a cooperative society which makes efficient use of its resources. If there is coercion in a society, then this cooperative system breaks down because the individual that is in the best place to make a decision is not allowed to do so. The decision is made by someone less knowledgeable or less informed, and the outcome is therefore less efficient. So then, coercion not only results in a loss of the freedom that people value, but also wastes the talent and knowledge of individuals, thus making society worse off than it would have been otherwise.

Lord Acton, the famous nineteenth-century English moralist and historian, is known for saying that power tends to corrupt, and absolute power corrupts absolutely. But it is not power itself that corrupts, but the power to coerce. There is a growing literature on what is meant by power, but for our particular point think of the ability of a company's chief executive officer to ensure that the company's product is produced in the most efficient manner. This sort of power does not lead to corruption, but rather to more products for consumers and cheaper prices. It may also lead to more employment opportunities for laborers. A producer cannot force people to work for him, as some suppose. Only when government has a monopoly over employment opportunities, such as in a planned economy, is a person forced to accept a particular type of employment regardless of his wishes. This power to coerce, where you must act according to the plans of another rather than your own, is what Acton meant when he described power as a corrupting influence.

Hayek believed that the purpose of government is to provide a social order that has the minimum amount of coercion. A social order without government results in a life described by Thomas Hobbes as "solitary, poor, nasty, brutish, and short." Freedom is best maintained, and the gains from individuals using their full capacity and knowledge, by limiting this governmental coercive power to the instances where it is needed to prevent other persons from coercing us. This, you recall, basically repeats what Bastiat says, that the role of government is to protect life, liberty, and property.

The interesting question is how this can best be accomplished. What sort of rules should we impose on that government to which we have granted this monopoly power of coercion? Does having a democratic government guarantee a system of free people? What are the responsibilities of individuals in a free society? It is to these questions that we now turn.

Chapter 9

CHARACTERISTICS OF A FREE SOCIETY: LAWS, DEMOCRACY, AND RESPONSIBILITY

Liberty is achieved by setting the strict conditions through which individuals grant the monopoly power of coercion to their government. These will be the rules of the game under which individuals will operate freely. The purpose here is not to list what the rules ought to be. That will be determined by the people living in the society in question. The purpose will be to present some guidelines of what the rule making process should be like. In doing this we will provide a path towards answering the questions posed at the end of the last chapter.

Characteristics of the Rules by Which Society is Governed

Hayek developed a set of characteristics of law that would minimize the chances of unbridled government coercion.[26] First, rules should be known by everyone. If the rules become so complicated and numerous that the average person cannot possibly know what they are, then the people will be at the mercy of those who enforce the rules. As an example, the current federal tax code is so lengthy and so open to interpretation, that I cannot possibly know all the tax law, even though one of my specialties is taxation policy. Surely the vast majority of persons who fill out their tax forms, or who do not fill out their tax forms, don't know all that is required of them under the tax code. What this means is that it is easy for a person who may decide to start a small business to unknowingly violate one of the provisions of the tax code. Or, for example, if you hire someone for more than $50 of work per three month period, which means hiring a student to be a babysitter for an evening once a week, then you must fill out some tax forms and withhold social security taxes on that person. How many people know about this, and how many actually do it? All of these persons could be prosecuted by their government, facing possible fines and/or jail sentences. This means that the government could, if it wanted to, prosecute vast numbers of the population. By having so many laws and so complicated a legal system that we cannot know when we are in violation of these laws, we live constantly at the mercy of those who enforce the laws. As James Madison put it more than two centuries ago:

> It will be of little avail to the people that laws are made by men of their own choice if the laws be so voluminous that they cannot be read, or so incoherent that they cannot be understood; or if they be repealed or

---

[26] See *The Constitution of Liberty*, op cit..

revised before they are promulgated, or undergo such incessant changes that no man who knows what the law is today, can guess what it will be like tomorrow.[27]

As a corollary to our first proposition, rules should also be predictable. People should be able to know what the law is, but they also should be able to predict what the law might be in the future. This allows individuals to plan ahead. The rules of the game shouldn't be changed frequently in a fashion that could not have been expected.

For example, suppose a businesswoman decides to invest in a machine that makes artificial cedar shingles for houses. This decision could be made a disaster by a government rule that outlawed artificial shingles three months after her investment. Arbitrary changes in the law therefore reduce people's incentives to take risks in their decision making and also direct persons into spending their resources influencing what the rules might be (this is what lobbyists are paid to do) rather than simply operating freely within existing rules.

Another characteristic of rules is that individuals should be able to comply with them. If the government were to pass a law that persons could not eat, then all of the society would become a criminal. This would allow the government to pick those it chooses to prosecute and subject them to various penalties. In this way the government would have the power to coerce any individual for any reason it might choose.

Rules should also be general in nature, that is, they should not apply to particular individuals or circumstances where it can be foreseen who will benefit or lose by the rules. The idea is that the law should be like the decision in the game Monopoly about what to do when someone lands on Free Parking. Some people play the way Parker Brothers intended, that Free Parking is simply a space where no rent is charged. Others play so that fines from Community Chest and Chance go into Free Parking and the first person to land on Free Parking gets the money. Deciding which way to play should be done before the game starts, so that we don't know that Wyatt will land on Free Parking more than Liam, and choose the rule that favors Wyatt. This is a prescription that is violated every day by both the federal congress and your state legislature. As Hayek puts it: "The law will prohibit killing another person or killing except under conditions so defined that they may occur at any time or place, but not the killing of particular persons."[28] Very often a law is passed because an individual or firm wishes to preclude some competitor from doing something, or wants to have the government transfer money to them or their cause. It is known specifically who benefits and loses when a law is passed and the law is made for particular people.

---

[27] The Federalist No. 62, *The Federalist Papers* (1787, New York: Bantam Books, 1982), p 317.
[28] *The Constitution of Liberty*, op cit.., p 152.

A truly free society would not be one where the government is able to use its coercive powers to assist or persecute specific individuals.

A free society requires that the rules apply equally to all people in similar circumstances. This is a basic concept of fairness that we all can relate to. We are always irritated at persons when "the law doesn't apply to them." If the local politician parks his car in a "no parking" zone and the parking control officer does not give him a ticket, then we are justifiably angered. But the reasoning behind this guideline goes beyond fairness. It ensures that those in the government who determine and enforce the laws cannot use the government's coercive force on a select few. If your company is precluded from producing an automobile that does not have air bags, then no company should be able to legally produce an automobile that does not have air bags.

If the rules allow government to pass laws that apply only to a minority, then it will be easier for government to be coercive. If I am not affected directly by a law, I am less likely to make and effort to oppose it. Slavery is unlikely to be passed as a law, for example, if anyone can be made a slave.

Legal vs. Legitimate

When these guidelines are followed in the rule-making process, then there will be a sphere of activity in which individuals can freely operate without the threat of coercion, either by individuals or by their government. This allows persons to use their resources and knowledge to advance their position and to adapt to changing circumstances.

However, being able to do something without coercion, i.e., without someone forcing you to do something else, does not mean all actions that you are free to do should meet with approval. Persons can be quite free to disapprove, morally, ethically, or for some other reason, with what you are doing. They are free to use the pressure of opinion in order to influence your behavior. They simply cannot threaten you with force.

This point is often missed in discussions regarding the consumption of illegal drugs. While you may feel that government should not be allowed to use its coercive force to disallow the use of crack cocaine, you certainly may use your persuasion in order to convince persons not to use cocaine, or to not associate with those who do use cocaine. You may choose as an employer not to hire persons who fail a drug test. It may be your moral responsibility to argue against the use of cocaine. The fact that you feel that the coercive force of government should not extend into the realm of limiting people's consumption of certain items does not mean that you must or do approve of their consumption of such items.

This is related to the idea mentioned earlier: should you be free to do whatever is not specifically forbidden by law, or should everything be precluded except that which is delineated by the rulers? Clearly, in a society based upon the former proposition, an action that is legal is not necessarily an action that is morally correct or that is legitimate in the eyes of society. Restricting government to using the minimum of coercion necessary to prohibit coercion of individuals by others will necessarily allow a vast amount of activity that the average citizen would not condone. Legalization therefore does not imply legitimization. Ignoring this precept has resulted in public policy regarding a number of activities that fails to solve problems, and that unnecessarily expands the coercive power of government. The failed experiment of Prohibition quickly comes to mind, where government's attempt to criminalize the drinking of alcohol, resulted in turning the alcoholic beverage industry over to organized crime; the taxation of certain products, such as cigarettes and beer, which primarily adds to the tax burden of the lower income; and in many states gambling is not allowed unless the government has a monopoly over the game.

In each of these cases, those who believe the activity is not legitimate have used the coercive power of government to prevent people from acting as they otherwise would have. Having failed in attempts to persuade people that something is immoral or harmful (or perhaps not even having attempted this route), various groups have used the power of government to force their views on others. While the belief that one should not smoke crack cocaine may be correct, it is up to those holding that view to persuade others to stop smoking it. When coercion is used rather than persuasion, freedom is reduced and a precedent for further coercion is established.

Democracy as a Means to an End

The second question with which we concluded the last chapter was this: Does a democratic government ensure a free society? The answer is no. Having the ability to participate in the choice of government or in the process of legislation does not necessarily result in individual liberty. A free people in this sense is not necessarily a nation of free individuals. The United States has a democratic republic, a political system which most people loosely term a democracy. Yet a casual study of its laws would find that they do not fit the guidelines that are necessary for a free society.

Hayek noted that the rules that delineate the boundary within which an individual may operate without coercion are called laws. The legislative body makes the laws and the executive branch enforces these laws. In a democracy, the majority either chooses the representatives who make the laws, or they make the laws themselves. Many states allow for both. In the state of Michigan, for example, the legislature is made up of the House of Representatives and the Senate. Members of the two houses of the legislature are elected by majority rule, and the legislature can and does pass legislation. However, the citizens of the state may also pass legislation through the initiative process. If enough signatures are gathered and the legislature does not directly pass the initiated law, the proposal is placed on the ballot where the voters determine through majority vote whether the initiative becomes law.

In a democracy the majority of persons decide what a law is. However, this does not mean that any particular law is just simply because a majority of people voted for it. Democracy is a means of determining what the law is, not a justification for a law having been made. As an example, suppose there are ten of us living on an island. We decide that our society will be run in a democratic fashion. I propose a law that the six of us who are males may enslave the four of us who are females. The six males then vote yes and the four females vote no, and thus the law passes. Are there many of us who would think that such a law were just? Yet it was made in a democratic fashion.

Often we are lead to believe that democracy is equivalent to freedom. Clearly it is not. Yet the media has harped on the question of whether the former Eastern European countries are now democratic, using "democratic" as a synonym for "free." These societies will be free when the laws that are established protect individuals from coercion, whether that coercion be by a single individual acting alone, or by a group of individuals using the power of government by majority rule.

The key to a free society is how to limit the power of temporary majorities. This can be done by establishing a long-term principle to which the members of society agree. Hayek says that a group becomes a society not by giving itself laws, but by obeying the same rules of conduct. This is consistent with Bastiat's position that morality is necessary for a just system of laws. If there is no general consensus about a law, or at least the reasoning behind a law, then that law will be impossible to enforce. Anyone who has read about the Volstead Act and the era of Prohibition in the United States can recognize that Bastiat is correct.

Bastiat argues that the question of universal suffrage is not as interesting when government is restricted to making just laws, those laws that protect life, liberty, and property. While there may be particular circumstances that fall in a gray area, there will not be enormous stakes involved. On the other hand, when government can make laws that take from one person and give to another, or can force you to purchase one person's product and prohibit you from purchasing another person's product, then it becomes important who is in the legislature and who votes for that legislature.

Hayek makes somewhat the same point. He contends that it is not obvious that universal suffrage is required by some basic principle. Articles in the literature of public choice have demonstrated that one can get the same outcome from a proper sampling of voters as from requiring all persons to vote. Anyone with a smattering of statistics can see the point here. One can gather a representative sample of the 150 million eligible voters and guarantee the outcome will mimic the result that would have occurred had all 150 million voted.

Even if all people are allowed to vote, a relevant question is how large the territory that will be the decision-making unit should be. Should everyone in Michigan vote on an issue that effects only the people in one county? Should Lithuanians vote on whether Latvians should restrict nuclear power plants? These are interesting questions which are related to the issue of universal suffrage. We should not take it for granted that there is some obvious reason that everyone should vote on every issue.

Once we have established that a group decision is necessary, then democracy is the proper means of arriving at that decision. When is a group decision necessary? When one opinion must prevail. As an example, suppose we have formed a recreational club to which we pay dues. These dues are then used to purchase a swimming pool. The location of the swimming pool is a natural group decision. The pool cannot be located at more than one place, so someone's opinion about where the pool is to be located must prevail.

Democracy becomes the means to the end of making the decision about where the pool should be. A primary reason that democracy is the proper means to reach the decision is it is much less wasteful than fighting. If there were two potential sites, we could divide our membership up and let the leaders of the two factions fight a duel, or we could have some type of gang fight with the winning side choosing the site. But voting is a much cheaper solution than any solution involving force.

Democracy is also more likely to promote liberty than other forms of government. Although the majority can still coerce the minority, there must be an opinion formed among a reasonably large percentage of the populace to allow that coercion to occur. A dictatorship places the government's monopoly power of coercion in one person. There may be periods when this person opposes coercion, but there may be other persons who become dictators who do believe in coercion. The incentives for this type of person to seek the dictatorship are strong, and thus the history of dictatorships has not been one of individual liberty.

Democracy only makes sense if you have a society in which you are free to influence the thinking of others. There is nothing inherent in a majority opinion that makes it correct. You may have a profound respect for the concept for majority rule, but have strong doubts that the majority is going to be correct in its decision about a particular issue. The responsible citizens must then attempt to influence the majority. But this can only happen if there is freedom of speech. Recall Mises' point that there is no line that divides economic freedoms and other freedoms. Freedom of speech is necessary both to economic freedom and to political freedom.

Individual Responsibility

The final question we raised at the finish of Chapter 8 dealt with the responsibility of the individual in a free society. Having liberty means that we must also accept the consequences of our actions. Recall that liberty is freedom from coercion, being able to make decisions about what we are going to do in our particular circumstance. If we are free to decide what to do, then we must live with the result of our action.

A free society offers choices. It does not guarantee results. You have the choice of deciding whether or not you wish to attempt to become an opera singer. If you misjudge your talent, or people's willingness to pay for your performance, then you must accept that result. You may starve and end up driving a taxicab. Then you may feel you have wasted all the years of training or listening to opera music. That is what freedom entails: no guarantees other than the freedom to make your own choices.

A free society demands that its people be guided by this sense of individual responsibility. When people are allowed to act as they see fit, people must believe that the outcomes that result from that action are the responsibility of the individual. This must be more than a legal concept. It must be more akin to a moral concept. It must be one of those general principles by which the society organizes itself.

When people believe that individuals are responsible for their own actions, it will also have an effect on individual behavior. It will make people choose in a fashion that would be different than if they felt they could not be held responsible. It requires them to prepare more, to make more efficient choices about the use of resources. When deciding whether to produce a certain product and thus use up resources in production, you will make sure that the value of those resources in other uses doesn't exceed the value in the use you make of them. If the value is greater in other uses, then you will have paid more to produce your product than you receive for it, and you will go bankrupt. Since this results in a reduction in your standard of living, you will be more careful than if the system is such that you are not held responsible for your choice, e.g., where the government reimburses you for any losses you incur.

This sense of responsibility also provides a moral justification for the manner in which society is organized. When we know that in a market system the distribution of income is actually determined by consumers, and that individuals can garner and maintain wealth only by pleasing consumers, it affects our attitude about the redistribution of income. In the same way, a sense that individuals are responsible for their actions results in a certain belief about the justice of the system.

Take that famous socialist utopia novel of the late nineteenth century by Edward Bellamy, *Looking Backward 2000-1877*.[29] In it Bellamy describes the economic system of late nineteenth-century Europe as a carriage ride in which certain people randomly end up in the driver's seat, and others randomly fall off into the mud and are then engaged in pulling the carriage. The idea is that it is primarily luck that determines the distribution of income in a capitalist society. If that is what you believe, then you probably believe that it is rather unfair that some people are rich and others are poor, since they do not become that way because of the results of their choices and actions. This means that a society should be able to form a government in which the government can take away from those who are rich and give to those who are poor.[30]

In a society where people are not held responsible for their actions, criminal activity is blamed on the circumstances or genetic characteristics of individuals. The belief that people who commit crimes do so by making rational choices and that they are accountable for these actions results in a much different view of criminal activity and the way society would deal with it.

Notice also that freedom is important for the altruistic individual as well as the person who seeks only personal gratification. One can hardly be considered altruistic when contributing to a cause under the threat of imprisonment. Unless you are free to choose not to contribute to a charity, and unless people believe that you are responsible for the good that occurs from your contribution, there is no room for altruism. The belief that it is a moral responsibility to volunteer one's time, treasure, and talent to the benefit of those less fortunate goes away. In a perfectly egalitarian society, there would be little altruism and a good deal of coercion.

In a free society, there is no guarantee that native ability or intelligence or education will lead to success. In a market economy, the use to which you put your talents and resources determines what your fortune will be. If you are lazy or make incorrect choices, then you will not be as successful as a person with less talent or resources that works harder or makes better choices. This sense of insecurity is what causes people to trade liberty for guarantees. There are risks involved in my accepting responsibility for my action. People can respond to this by giving up their freedom in order to sustain some minimum result.

---

[29] *Looking Backward 2000-1887* (Boston: Houghton, Mifflin and Company,1886)

[30] It also presumes that people will not respond to this situation by behaving in such a way that will reduce the amount of goods and services available.

How do we ensure that a procedure of creating laws is likely to result in a free society? How do we articulate the general principle that society will follow? How can we ensure that our political system does not drift toward a coercive one? In the next chapter we will see that the advent of the written constitution provided an anchor to hold the ship of state in the bay of liberty.

Chapter 10

```

```

PRESERVING FREEDOM:
THE CONSTITUTION

In 1767 the British Parliament issued a declaration that parliament could enact any law it saw fit as long as the majority of parliament voted in favor of it. This declaration was important because it said there was no constraint upon any temporary majority that happened to control the parliament. The concept that laws passed by parliament would have to conform to a set of general principles embodied in a constitution had yet to be established.

Some of the American colonial leaders, such as James Otis, Samuel Adams, and Patrick Henry, objected to the declaration of parliament because it would allow legislatures to do anything they pleased as long as a majority consented. However, Britain did not have a written constitution with which the colonists could challenge parliament. The American colonists concluded that they needed a written document that could serve as a foundation for their colonial society, a written constitution that would set limits on what the elected government could and could not do.

Their idea was to establish a strictly constrained representative government. The constitution would serve as the document that established the basic principles under which their society would be governed. These principles would be put into action by granting certain powers to the legislative body while reserving all other powers to the people. The expression "all power to the people," so often used and misused throughout our lives, was intended by those who wrote the Constitution to establish the precept that the people could bind their legislative body.

The Constitution as a General Principle

According to Hayek, the American colonies were the first to put into writing the concept of a higher law directing the establishment of the laws that governed everyday life. Of course, over the centuries several writers have suggested that there is a higher authority than man or a man-made institution.

The suggestions for a higher authority include God, Nature, and Reason. But the point is that no previous society had a written document setting forth the principles that would limit their legislative body's authority to create laws.

A constitution is very different from an ordinary law because it binds the legislature when that body is making particular laws. This means that the legislature should be constrained from altering the constitution. Otherwise, a constitution could be amended whenever the legislative body felt constrained, and thus the document would not serve its function. As a constitution reflects the basic beliefs of society, it should be established and amended only by the citizenry at large if and when that citizenry has altered its basic principles.

If the legislature does not follow any general principles when passing legislation, it will inadvertently establish such principles in an ad hoc fashion. Thus, any time a situation arises similar to something that has happened in the past, it will be difficult for legislators to vote differently than they did the first time. As an example, suppose the automobile dealers association gets a law passed which says that auto companies must buy back any unsold inventory from auto dealers. When the lobbyist for the boat dealers association shows up at the legislator's fund raiser, it will be hard for the legislator to refuse to support a bill that would require boat companies to buy back unsold inventories from their dealers. Next, in will come the lobbyists for the farm implement dealers, the book dealers, and all other dealers one can think of. The principle will have been inadvertently established that the government should set the terms of contracts between producers and their dealers.

A constitution establishes the general principle that is agreed upon by the majority of the population and which binds all future majorities until such time that the majority no longer agrees with one of the basic principles. The majority that existed in the past binds the current majority in the legislative branch. This entails a division of authority between those who write and approve of the constitution and those who make laws based upon the constitution. It presupposes that there is a recognition of generally accepted principles over ad hoc solutions to problems, and that there is an underlying agreement in society of what these generally accepted principles are.

Power is thus maintained not by physical force, but by the underlying agreement of the members of society. This was pointed nearly 450 years ago when Etienne de La Boetie wrote *The Discourse of Voluntary Servitude*.[31] In this little book, written about the time Machiavelli was writing *The Prince*, Boetie ponders why people allow themselves to be ruled by dictators. A ruler can only maintain power as long as the majority of people allow him to use that power. In the short run, military force may keep someone in power, but in the long run a person or government can maintain power only by having the acceptance of those ruled. In the same fashion, a constitution documents the commonly accepted principles and limits under which the power of government is to be exercised.

Limitations placed upon a temporary majority are not undemocratic. Rather, they preserve democracy by protecting the people against those who have been granted the power of coercion. The limitations written down in a constitution determine the order of society. Hayek calls the United States Constitution a

---

[31] *The Politics of Obedience: The Discourse of Voluntary Servitude* (1552, New York: Free Life, 1975)

"constitution of liberty", because it protects the individual against arbitrary coercion by the government.

The Ninth Amendment: Judicial Power and Legislative Constraint

The Bill of Rights, the first ten amendments to the United States Constitution, creates a puzzle. In the last chapter we noted that there is a difference between the situation where an individual is free to do anything unless specifically barred from so doing, and the case where an individual is free to do only what is granted. In the same fashion, there is a difference between a situation where the government is free to do anything not specifically prohibited by a constitution, or the situation where the government may do only those things which are expressly granted by the constitution. When the ratification of the Constitution was debated, one group felt it was necessary to include a Bill of Rights, as was included in some state constitutions, in order to ensure that the new federal government could not pass laws that infringed on basic liberties. Another group felt that a Bill of Rights was unnecessary because the Constitution did not provide the federal government with the power to infringe on these liberties in the first place. This group felt that by placing a Bill of Rights in the Constitution it would be implying that the federal government had powers that went beyond those specifically enumerated in the body of the Constitution. The Ninth and Tenth Amendments[32] were meant to address this concern. They reserve rights that were not specifically enumerated to the individuals and the states.

Hayek's primary concern involves constructing a political system that allows a democratic method for settling disputes when one outcome must prevail, while at the same time protecting the individual from coercion by the majority. The Ninth Amendment is one of the most important amendments in his view, as it establishes that the rights of individuals go beyond those enumerated in the Constitution. The entire text of the amendment is:

> The enumeration in the Constitution of certain rights shall not be construed to deny or disparage others retained by the people.

This implies that the legislative branch is not free to do whatever it wants. Rather, there are other rights of individuals—possibly numerous—which may not be infringed upon by an activist legislature. In *The Constitution of Liberty*, Hayek bemoans the weakening of the Ninth Amendment, or the outright ignoring of it, by the U.S. Supreme Court over the years. He writes that the weakening of the Ninth

---

[32] There were actually twelve amendments presented by Madison as part of the Bill of Rights. Ten were ratified in 1791. One of the other two, the one precluding congress from passing a pay raise during a current term, was finally ratified in 1992.

Amendment has led to legislation that goes well beyond what the Constitution intended to allow and has lessened our individual liberty.

This interpretation of the Ninth Amendment is not universal, even among those who are concerned with the protection of individual liberty. There has been a good deal of controversy in recent years regarding the broadening of power of the judicial branch. Some scholars, such as Robert Bork and Supreme Court Justice Antonin Scalia, believe that the judiciary has taken to interpreting the Constitution in such a way as to allow them to actually legislate.[33] Their fear is not that a runaway legislature may infringe upon individual liberty, but rather that a runaway judicial branch will threaten individual liberty. Interpreting the Ninth Amendment in the way envisioned by Hayek could allow the judicial branch to create all sorts of individual rights that could then be used to strike down legislation or reach decisions that have the force of legislation.

One of the primary recent examples of this is the establishment of the "right of privacy" in *Griswold v. Connecticut* in 1965.[34] This decision was then used in *Roe v. Wade* (1973) to strike down certain state prohibitions against abortion.[35] The argument made by Bork, and others, is not about the moral aspects of abortion. Their concern is that by broadly interpreting the Constitution, even finding things that are not written in it, the judicial branch effectively removed the power of legislating the abortion issue from the legislative branch. As there is no appeal from the judicial branch, the threat to individual liberty from judicial activism is greater than the threat to individuals from the legislative branch.

Of course, there is no clear consensus on this broader issue of judicial activism, of which the Ninth Amendment is only a narrow part. Hamilton, in the Federalist Paper #78, wrote:

> Whoever attentively considers the different departments of power must perceive, that, in a government in which they are separated from each other, the judiciary, from the nature of its functions, will always be the least dangerous branch to the political rights of the Constitution. [36]

Indeed, the ability of the Supreme Court to strike down laws of the Congress that are in violation of the Constitution is not explicitly found in the document. This power was established by Chief Justice John Marshall in *Marbury v. Madison* (1803). Yet today, scholars and judges who are concerned with judicial activism feel that the expanding power of the judiciary threatens the very foundation of our social order.

---

[33] A good place to begin a study of this controversy is Robert Bork's book, *The Tempting of America*, (New York:: Macmillan, 1990)

[34] *Griswold v. Connecticut*, 381 U.S. 479.

[35] *Roe v. Wade*, 410 U.S. 113.

[36] *The Federalist Papers*, op cit., p. 393.

The underlying issue here is the power to coerce. We have defined freedom as the ability to act on our own wishes with the minimum feasible amount of coercion. We have shown that a society ordered upon such a principle will have the most efficient method of allocating resources, and result in the highest standard of living. The purpose of the Constitution is to ensure that each individual is protected from coercion by an organized majority. Does the Constitution best fulfill its purpose through an interpretation of its precepts by the judiciary that sticks only to what is actually written, and thus presuming that the legislative branch may do whatever is not specifically prohibited in writing? Or, does the Constitution best serve its purpose through a broad interpretation of its precepts by the judiciary, allowing the judicial branch considerable power over the legislative branch? These are important questions that the average person ignores only at his or her peril. As Mises says about economics, these are issues too important to be left to the intellectual elite, for these issues determine the shape of our everyday life.

Chapter 11

PROGRESS

We have looked at the market system as a means of allocating resources and—in conjunction with a constitutional democracy—determining the social order. This system has a number of desirable characteristics including an efficient use of resources, an income distribution determined by way of pleasing consumers, and a maximum of individual freedom. We have indicated that the market system will lead to a high standard of living. In the next three chapters we will use history as a tableau for gaining a perspective on how wealthy we really are and how we got that way: we will put forth the basic requirements for progress, and then briefly scan the history of the western world from the medieval period to the present to see important aspects of different periods which encouraged economic growth. In Chapter 13 we will go one step further and offer lessons from history to poor countries wishing to increase their standard of living, and to wealthy countries that are endangering their own standard.

Of Axes and Cavemen

Let's think about how the first axe came about.[37] A caveman is wandering about the ancient world being chased by mastodons, living off of whatever he can gather from available plants, and eating what few animals he can capture, perhaps a wounded wooly mammoth or two. Then, he gets the idea that rather than using his hands or a randomly gathered rock to dig up the berries or finish off the wooly mammoth and skin it, a tool would be useful: an axe. However, making the axe, perhaps first a prototype and then a working axe, will have an opportunity cost. The opportunity cost here is time. In order to build the axe, he must spend time that he could otherwise have spent grubbing for roots and finding wounded animals.

Suppose that anyone could take the axe as soon as it was finished. Then our caveman would have no axe and no food. There would be no incentive to develop and produce the axe. In order for the axe to be invented and built, there must be some system of property rights. The caveman must know that in giving up the time that could be spent foraging for food, he will obtain an axe that he can use to improve future food foraging. Sole property rights to the axe are vital.

---

[37] This example, as well as some of the discussion of the role of individualism in this chapter, was inspired by an interesting little book by Henry Grady Waver, *The Mainspring of Human Progress*, 2nd edition (Irvington-on-Hudson: The Foundation for Economic Education, 1953).

Once property rights to tools have been established, our caveman may decide that he is better at making axes than at killing mastodons. He then builds axes for other cave people and swaps them for mastodon meat. He may give up foraging and hunting altogether to concentrate on axe-making. This specialization of labor and peaceful exchange of goods forms a foundation for economic progress. Specialization of labor is so important for progress that Adam Smith begins his famous *An Inquiry Into the Nature and Causes of the Wealth of Nations* with the statement:

> The greatest improvement in the productive powers of labor, and the greater part of the skill, dexterity, and judgment with which it is any where directed, or applied, seem to have been the effects of the division of labor. [38]

As indicated in our example, in order for this specialization to occur, not only must there be well-defined property rights, but also an institutional mechanism for the exchange of goods and services. Obviously, there must be some agreed-upon method by which the caveman may trade his second axe for fifty pounds of mastodon meat. This mechanism for trade is most fully developed in the market system that we have spent so much time analyzing. In *The Wealth of Nations*, Smith describes how interrelated a system of trade becomes under specialization of labor. He begins with the woolen coat worn by one of the common laborers and notices how it is the product of the shepherd, the wool-comber, the dyer, the spinner, the weaver, the fuller, the dresser, etc. and how each of these persons must "join their different arts in order to complete even this homely production."[39]

Individualism

A system of property rights and trade is what we might think of as rules or institutions that must develop in order for progress to occur. But there must also be a general attitude that the individual matters and is capable of affecting the outcome of events. This attitude provides the incentive for invention and innovation, and the spark of thought that leads to progress.

Imagine living in an ancient pagan society where the tribe is the most important unit of life. Each individual exists only in order to support the life of the tribe. This is akin to the belief that the primary role of individual members of a species is to further the existence of the species as a whole. For example, in this primitive society we might believe in human sacrifice. Since the tribe is more important than any individual, we could put you on an altar to the sun god and cut

---

[38] (Indianapolis: Liberty Classics, 1981), vol. 1, p.13.

[39] Ibiid., p 22.

your head off in order to induce the sun god to make the weather good for planting our crops. Knowing that you might be sacrificed at any time for the good of the tribe, your incentives for inventing things depend upon your allegiance to the tribe. You benefit from your invention only to the extent that the tribe is better off and you have some share in the extra goods that now will exist. However, you might also become so valuable that you make the most pleasing sacrifice at the next sun god festival.

Of course, some people will become excited about the tribe and will work hard to improve it. But if we really examine our inner feelings, most of us know that, while we are willing to do things for the tribe, we are more likely to be interested in doing things for ourselves. It took 6000 years for civilization to get to the point where men had a two-wheel cart. From Moses to George Washington civilization managed to get to a four-wheel cart. During this period, most societies were based upon the belief that individuals are less important than the tribe or the society. The slow pace of progress might indicate that societies based upon the importance of the tribe over the individual do not spur innovation.

Another attitude necessary to foster advancement is that individuals are capable of affecting events and are responsible for their own actions. This is what we discussed earlier in Chapter 9 in the context of a free society. For thousands of years people believed that individuals were not responsible for improving their own lives, and that some overriding authority was. This authority could be a supernatural figure, as an ancient Greek god, or a human being with divine powers, such as an Egyptian pharaoh. Human initiative was stymied by this belief that individuals have no control of their own destiny and, unless they were a mythical hero, just went along for the ride. Even heroes were forced into situations by gods and often got out of them only through the help of other gods. The result was very little progress.

Today we are used to vast advances in technology and standards of living. Just as an example, my grandmother was born before the invention of the airplane. There were no cars in her hometown when she was very young. She was a mother by the time television was invented. Yet before she died, she could watch the landing of the space shuttle on a 40-inch flat screen color television with remote control and surround-sound, except for the fact that space shuttle landings are now so common that they are not even covered in the news. We expect that these references to modern technology will seem terribly outdated when reading this book ten years from now. Yet we need to put this in perspective. The Egyptians invented sailing ships in 3200 BC. Approximately 5000 years later, people were still using sailing ships as the major means of transporting goods. Try to imagine what the primary means of transportation will be 500 years from now, much less 5000 years from now.

It has only been in the last few hundred years that large portions of society have lived in a world where both the institutions of property rights and market transactions are dominant, where people have a belief in the importance of the individual and in the individual's ability to improve his or her life, and where people have the responsibility for doing so. Prior to this situation, progress was slow and fitful. Today, in areas of the world where the belief that the individual is subservient to society and exists for the benefit of society as a whole, progress still lags.

Individuals, not societies, produce and progress. The purpose of human society is to allow individual exchange, cooperation, and protection of life, liberty, and property. Thinking that the individual can be sacrificed for the common good not only impedes economic growth, it also is dangerous. It leads to tyranny, dictatorship, and wholesale slaughter. Could the killing of millions of people during World War II and the period following it, as well as the current slaughter of thousands of persons in struggling African nations occur if everyone recognized the importance of the individual? Could any country begin a war without an appeal to that country's individuals to sacrifice themselves or their friends for the good of the society? In his book written between the two world wars, *Liberalism in the Classical Tradition*, Ludwig von Mises made a vain appeal to the world to adopt the philosophy of classical liberal thought as a means of averting the coming Second World War.[40] He pointed out with great clarity that a social order based upon individualism and free exchange is not consistent with armed aggression. Such a society not only leads to economic progress, but also to world peace.

When individual initiatives are not allowed to emerge, the inevitable outcome is poverty and economic stagnation. This, in turn, leads to internal violence and aggression at both national and regional levels. The urban violence that we witness in the United States today may be at least partially explained by a social order which has given up the belief in property rights and the importance of the individual and his ability and responsibility to affect his own destiny. With this has come the effective abandonment of certain areas by the market system, leading to further economic decline and breakdown of the social order.

Progress lies in working in harmony with the fundamental nature of man. This does not mean a society based upon tribal beliefs where subservient members of the tribe are passively resigned to whatever the gods bestow upon them. Nor does it mean the modern day equivalent: the planned economy where an "authority" determines which occupation each individual may engage in and what is produced for whom and in what fashion. Such social orderings result in economic stagnation. This does not mean that they are necessarily unstable,

---

[40] (Irvington-on-Hudson: The Foundation for Economic Education and Cobden Press, 1985). This book was first published in 1927.

although these conditions can lead to political instability. Sparta lasted for more than 400 years. During that time they had numerous wars. However, those Spartans living in Sparta in 700 BC and those living in Sparta in 350 BC had pretty much the same lifestyle. Four hundred years of their society did not lead to the invention of the sleep-easy mattress. As for their standard of living, life was almost exactly the same for centuries.

The point is that humans innovate and produce best when they are free to act according to their own wills and are responsible for their actions. A social ordering based upon this facet of human nature will lead to progress. The United States has enjoyed such a social ordering for most of its existence. This has resulted in the enormous progress we have today. Over the last seventy years, however, American society has gradually moved away from the social ordering most compatible with economic progress. While we may wish to trade off progress for certain other things, this decision is best made explicitly by an informed populace. Each of us must be aware of the consequences of individual government policies upon the institutional structure and the attitudes and values of the citizenry, and what effect these have, in turn, on our standard of living.

Chapter 12

A HISTORICAL OUTLINE OF
WESTERN PROGRESS

This chapter offers a very brief outline of the economic progress of the Western world, based upon *How the West Grew Rich* by Birdzell and Rosenberg.[41] The intent is neither to provide a specific history of each area within Western civilization, nor to describe in detail the critical events of each period. Rather, the intent is to spur the reader to contemplate the general trends in economic development and to relate them to the dominant social and political structure of different historical periods in an effort to determine what creates economic growth. After reading this chapter you might view your further readings in history in a slightly different light.

Economic growth occurs over time through innovation and the gradual accumulation of what is generally termed capital goods. Innovation, the creative use of the human mind and talent in order to develop new products, tools, methods of organization, scientific discovery, etc., is the primary mechanism of advancement. Societies that foster innovation (those with well-defined property rights, a mechanism for exchange, and a belief in the importance of the individual) will outperform societies that do not. Capital goods are machinery, equipment, and buildings, as well as improved human resources, such as education and training. Societies with a stock of capital will be wealthier than societies with less capital.

In examining the history of the Western world we will focus on aspects of each stage from the feudal period to the present that have fostered innovation and capital accumulation. This overview should provide those countries seeking to advance from a subsistence state with knowledge on how to spur economic growth, and a warning for developed countries that are in danger of retarding economic growth due to recent political trends and changes in values.

Feudal Period: 900-1450

We will begin with the feudal period, which for our purposes is from approximately 900 to 1450 A.D. Of course, there existed a great variety of conditions across the European world of this time. However, certain generalizations are accurate enough to give us a flavor of the era. The three major points to keep in mind are: (1) feudal society was overwhelmingly agricultural; (2) political and economic authority were generally combined in the same institution,

---

[41] Nathan Rosenberg and L.E. Birdzell, *How the West Grew Rich: The Economic Transformation of the Industrial World* (New York: Basic Books, 1986).

the manor in the countryside and the guild in the towns; and (3) the terms of exchange were set by custom and law and not through negotiated prices.

Most people in a feudal society were preoccupied with raising or finding enough food to eat. They did not spend a great deal of time working on their snowmobiles or jet skis or playing video games. Life was basic and hard. One worked from light until dark attempting to raise or find food. Aside from some folks who were employed in the towns as artisans or apprentices, or those who became merchants, people lived in an agricultural setting.

The primary social ordering of the time was the manor system.[42] While this system varied throughout the western world, we can make some generalizations. The manor was a self-sufficient unit based upon an agricultural system, basically a farm with the lord of the manor in charge. The peasants, or serfs, lived in small villages under the protection of the lord of the manor. The village was usually located in the vicinity of the manor walls. In return for the lord's protection, the serfs were essentially bound to the soil. This system was a form of servile labor and was called *adscripti glebae*. There were very few people who were really free. Serfs were not, for example, able to move from one village or manor to another at will. Usually they could not even marry without obtaining their lord's permission.

The serfs' primary occupation was tilling the manor land, a major portion of which was the land of the lord, called the lord's demesne. The serfs also tilled some land for themselves. This land was often in large open fields with each peasant holding several strips scattered throughout the field. This meant it made sense for the land to be farmed in common, the serfs working together to farm the whole plot rather than trying to plant and harvest scattered individual plots. In addition, if there was plowing to be done, it required several oxen. Since few peasants owned more than one or two oxen, the plowing was done in common. This was also true of the harvesting, with the animals grazing on the stubble.

In addition to working for the lord, the peasants owed taxes to the lords, tithes to the church, and royal taxes. Thus, the peasants' standard of living was sufficient to exist, but did not allow for improvements. The lord and his knights protected the peasant from the raids of war-like tribes, and the lord in turn was supported by the peasant labor.

There was little use of money in the manor system, as there was little need for exchange other than barter. Money was only needed for those items in which the manor was not self-sufficient. What exchange did occur was at compulsory or "just" prices and wages. There were few specialized traders. People generally traded the items that they had produced themselves. For example, the wife of a serf might make an extra shirt and trade it for some candles.

---

[42] For a brief exposition of the manor system see Rondo Cameron, *A Concise Economic History of the World* (Oxford: Oxford University Press, 1989), Ch 3.

An important thing to note about the feudal system is the power the lord of the manor had in both the political and economic sphere. The lord was not only the political power in the manor, but he also determined such things as how much land each peasant could till, how much of the produce each peasant was allowed to retain, what marriages would be allowed, where peasants could locate, etc. This power of the lord over the peasant in both the political and economic systems was a serious impediment to innovation and economic development.

While important agricultural innovations did occur during the feudal period (the introduction of the heavy-wheeled plow, the use of horses in agriculture, the introduction of iron in agricultural implements, and the use of crop rotation, for example), the rate of progress was certainly slow. The entire economic and political organization was based upon custom and tradition with little incentive for any person to innovate.

The towns which existed were dominated by the guild system. Guilds were essentially unions of merchants and craftsman that acted to set prices, production practices, market shares, and limit entry into the profession. Those who were the leaders of the guilds were able to determine whether you could live in the town and if you could engage in employment there. Like the manor lords, the guilds in the towns controlled not only the economic system, but the political system as well.

You can imagine what sort of incentives there were to innovate in a town organized under the guild system. If you decided you wanted to be a craftsman and produce a new product, or an old product in a new way, you had to get permission from those who were producing the old product in the old way. They were in power under the old system, and would be unlikely to want to rock the boat. The odds of you getting the chance to innovate were highly improbable. The most likely outcome would be that you had only created trouble for yourself.

In a world based upon tradition and custom, a world in which your occupation and where you lived were determined by tradition and the good wishes of the lord of the manor or the leaders of the guild, not much happened. As noted above, there were some advancements in agriculture. There were important inventions by medieval tinkerers and the introduction of items discovered in other parts of the world into Europe. These included the compass, the clock, eyeglasses, soapmaking, gunpowder, and water mills. However, the system was not one which encouraged or drove innovation. As a result, it is not far from the truth to say that if you were living on a manor in 1110, you did not expect things to be much different in 1150, or even 1220. The concept of imagining what the future was going to be like, and taking steps to be prepared for possible changes was relatively alien. If next year was going to be the same as this year, then why bother to plan for the future?

Just to get a feel for the rapidity of change, think of one of the late night movies on television, or maybe a big screen movie such as *Willow* or *The Princess*

Bride, that take place in the Medieval period. There will be knights and castles and perhaps dragons. Now, how often can you tell if the year being depicted in the movie is 1230, or 1375, or 980? Part of this is surely due to our ignorance of history (perhaps a rational ignorance given the opportunity cost of learning enough about the Middle Ages to spot subtle differences). But much of it is due to the fact that not much changed in that period. If you were watching a movie about Detroit, you could certainly tell if the year was 1950 or 2000, just by the type of cars driven, clothing styles, housing patterns. We live in a period where we expect rapid change and assume that life fifteen years from now will be significantly different from today. But if we had lived in medieval Europe, we would have assumed that things fifteen years from now would be pretty much like they are today.

Although the feudal period was one of slow growth and had few incentives for innovation for the vast majority of the populace, it contained the basis for the beginning of economic development: the diffusion of power across the various lords and towns, and the lack of a strong central authority to stop the rise of the merchant class and trading cities. Each lord had strong central authority over his own manor, and each town was dominated by the economic and political power of the guilds, but the towns and manors were only loosely organized together. Kings of the period were not absolute monarchs. They relied upon the lords for support. There was no equivalent of the Roman emperor who could command absolute power over vast tracts of land. As a consequence, Europe arrived at this new epoch of trade and expansion of world markets without a strong central authority to constrain the ability of the merchant class to seek out profits and develop their businesses.

During the feudal period, trading cities began to develop, particularly in Italy, that operated outside of the feudal system of lord-ruled manors and guild-dominated towns. By the year 1200 there were several city-states in northern Italy. This development of markets began in cities because an urban population cannot be as self-sufficient as a manorial system. The existence of trading centers and the expansion of the urban population began to put pressure on the old feudal way of life.

The feudal system reached its zenith around 1300, and remained a significant but declining factor for the next 150 years. The payment of money-wages to laborers and rent to landlords began to replace the servile labor system. As early as 1035, Milan shook itself from the feudal system. The rest of Italy, the Low Countries, the Rhineland, and northern France began to witness the development of these urban trade centers. By 1367 German cities and cities dominated by German merchants formed an organization of cities called the Hansa to protect trade routes and ensure freedom of trade.

It was because the feudal system was also a military system that changes in military tactics helped make feudalism obsolete. Knights on horseback had been the primary weapon, and the king relied on the support of the lords and knights to wage his battles. The lords and knights were paid by the king primarily through the granted use of the land. For the most part this was a barter arrangement. But the trading centers, especially in Italy, began instead to use professional armies to protect commerce. This sped up the use of money exchange and the introduction of money agriculture, where the peasants were paid for their produce with money. Professional armies were also more likely to compete against one another in the development of new weapons. Some of these weapons, such as siege cannons and crossbows, reduced the advantages of a military system based on castles and knights in armor.

With the decline of the barter economy and the rise of trade, money agriculture became more and more the *modus operandi*. Serfs were in turn paid for their labor, rather than simply retaining a portion of the crops. As this system developed, serfs began to purchase their way out of feudal obligations and to hold land.

The fourteenth century was unusually rough and marked the end of the feudal system. There was a great famine in the early part of the century. In 1348 an epidemic of bubonic plague hit Europe, and new outbursts occurred every fifteen to twenty years throughout the century. The population of Europe declined by about a third under these pressures. Serfs began to revolt, with uprisings occurring in Flanders in 1315, France in 1358, and England in 1381. Landlords competed with one another for the declining labor force. The idea that serfs were tied to the land dissolved in the aftermath of the severe labor shortage created by the famines, plagues, and civil unrest of the period.

By the beginning of the fifteenth century the feudal system in Western Europe had given way to a system of money agriculture, peasant landowners, and trading cities. A merchant class arose outside of the feudal system, free to trade at negotiated prices and to assume the risks and rewards of local and regional markets.

The key to this economic development rising from the feudal system was the diffusion of power among the manors and towns. As the feudal system began to collapse, there was no central authority capable of enforcing the status quo, or of limiting trade. The next period saw further development of trade and the enlargement of the class of individuals who were to determine their own destiny.

Comparative Advantage

Why should people trade? One obvious reason, as indicated above, is that specialization of labor results in greater output, and specialization of labor can only come about if people can trade. But what should we specialize in? Our intuition tells us that if I am better than you at painting and you are better at hanging wallpaper, then we could produce more if I painted and you wallpapered than if we both were self-sufficient in our home improvement. Our gut feeling is that people should specialize in those things that they do better than other people.

But what would happen if I can both wallpaper better and paint better than you? Our intuition this time might tell us that I am better off doing both my own painting and wallpapering and leaving you to your own slow devices. This, however, is not the case, as the English economist David Ricardo called attention to at the beginning of the nineteenth century.[43] It turns out that we will always be better off specializing and trading, even if I am better than you at everything or you are better than I am at everything. This important point is termed the law of comparative advantage. The key to understanding this law lies in the concept of opportunity cost.

Suppose you and I have identical houses. We are threatened by our wives with no television sports until we paint our respective bedrooms and wallpaper our bathrooms. It is the weekend before the Super Bowl, so we are ready for home-improvement action. It takes me two hours to paint the bedroom, and three hours to wallpaper the bathroom. It takes you, as you are relatively uncoordinated, three hours to paint the bedroom, and four hours to wallpaper the bathroom. Since I am faster at painting and wallpapering, I might be tempted to do my own painting and wallpapering. However, being an economist, I know that we will both be better off by specializing and trading services.

Why is this so, and what should I choose to specialize in? To answer these questions we need to look at my opportunity cost (as well as your opportunity cost, since you also need to know the answer). Let's call one unit of painting, completing a bedroom, and one unit of wallpapering completing a bathroom. Now we must look at the opportunity cost to me of one unit of painting. It takes me two hours to paint and three hours to wallpaper. So the two hours I spend painting could get me two-thirds of the way through a wallpaper job. Thus, the opportunity cost to me of one unit of painting is two-thirds of a unit of wallpapering. Now we can do the same thing for my opportunity cost of wallpapering. To finish a wallpapering job takes three hours, and with that three hours I could do one and one-half paint jobs. So to me, the opportunity cost of one unit of wallpapering is one and one-half units of painting.

Let us turn our attention to you. One unit of painting costs you three-fourths of a unit of wallpapering, since it takes you three hours to paint and four hours to wallpaper. One unit of wallpapering costs you one and one-third units of painting, since you could paint one and one-third bedroom units in the four hours it takes you to wallpaper.

---

[43] See his *Principles of Political Economy* (Amherst, New York: Prometheus, 1996), which was first published in 1817.

Opportunity Cost of Home Improvements		
Person	Painting	Wallpapering
Me	2/3 W	1 1/2 P
you	3/4 W	1 1/3 P

Table 12-1

Since the opportunity cost to me of painting is less than it is for you, and the opportunity cost of wallpapering is less for you than it is for me, I should specialize in painting and you should specialize in wallpapering. The intuitive reason is that although I am more efficient than you at both things, my efficiency advantage is greatest at painting. Because I am so good at painting, it costs me more to do something other than paint than it costs you. While I have an absolute advantage over you in both painting and wallpapering, I only have a comparative advantage over you in painting.

Notice that the opportunity cost to you of wallpapering is smaller than it is for me. Although it takes you longer to wallpaper than it does me, you give up less painting when you wallpaper than I do when I wallpaper. Your opportunity cost of a unit of wallpapering is one and one-third units of painting while mine is one and one-half units.

Let's see how this example works to make us both better off. Suppose that I follow the first route and decide to be a self-sufficient homeowner, painting my own bedroom and wallpapering my own bathroom. It would take me a total of five hours. Since I won't trade services with you, you are forced to paint and wallpaper your own home as well, taking seven hours. It takes us a total of twelve hours to get ready for the Super Bowl.

Instead, suppose we are armed with the knowledge of comparative advantage. You wallpaper for seven hours. This is the same amount of time that you would have spent doing your home by yourself. In this time you will have completed your home and three-fourths of mine. I paint both of our houses, taking four hours, and finish the one-fourth of my wallpapering job. The wallpapering will take me three-fourths of an hour. As it takes me three hours to wallpaper one full bathroom, it will take me three-fourths of an hour to do one-fourth of the job. By working together we have saved fifteen minutes of labor, since you work a total of seven hours and I work a total of four and three quarter hours. While fifteen minutes may not sound like it was worth all the bargaining necessary to make our deal, when the principle is applied to millions of workers doing millions of different jobs, the savings are enormous.

"But wait a minute!" you might say after thinking about this for a minute. "Why did you get all the benefit of this?" Only because I have made you a poor bargainer in setting the terms under which we traded labor. In practice, the traders will determine at what rate they are willing to trade in order to share the extra fifteen minutes. You might work a little less than seven hours and I work a little more than four and three-quarter hours. The point, however, is that there is a benefit to be shared between us from trading, even though I have an absolute advantage over you in both painting and wallpapering. This will always be true. It will always be the case that each party will have a comparative advantage in something because its opportunity costs cannot exceed the opportunity cost of the other party for everything.

David Ricardo developed the concept of comparative advantage to demonstrate that countries are always better off under a free trade situation. In fact, if you think about it from a common-sense point of view, even if one of our trading partners puts up barriers to trade, so trade is not "fair," we are better off not putting up barriers to their selling goods to us. That is because whenever there is an uncoerced trade, both sides must become better off. By limiting the number of possible trades, we are reducing the opportunities to gain.

The Expansion of Trade: 1450-1750

It is important to note that the time periods I have chosen are only for convenience. The feudal period did not end on December 31, 1449. There was a gradual development of the market system and a gradual decline of the manor system based upon subsistence agriculture. Also, these changes did not occur evenly throughout Europe or the world. The part of Europe that Russia occupies today remained a feudal system for hundreds of years after the feudal system had disappeared in the areas dominated by the Hansa cities. The periods have been chosen to make a point regarding what was generally the case in the Western world at different times.

The period from 1450 to 1750 saw a great expansion in commerce. While trading cities and substantial commerce existed during the Middle Ages, particularly toward the end of the feudal era, if one were to pick the most important economic feature of the three hundred years from the middle of the fifteenth century to the middle of the eighteenth century, it would be the expansion of trade.

Agriculture remained relatively stagnant, as did industrial production. Again, there were some advances. The invention of a simple stocking frame for knitwear increased by ten times the number of stitches that could be made. One of the greatest inventions of all time, printing with movable type, occurred in the fifteenth century. There were advancements in firearms and artillery, clock-making, and navigational instruments. Yet the pace of invention was still relatively slow.

The most significant advancements occurred where the economy was market oriented. Industry was carried out in the rudimentary market economy of the era. It was more market-based than agriculture, which, except for some notable exceptions such as the Low Countries, was still aimed at self-sufficiency. The ability of entrepreneurs to benefit directly from inventions was a primary reason for the advancement that did occur. However, since a local authority could regulate industry, it did not provide individuals the freedom that existed within trade and commerce. As an example, in 1551 the English Parliament passed a law that precluded the use of gig-mils, a device that allowed increased production in the cloth-finishing trade.[44] Laws such as this were passed to impede laborsaving devices because the authorities wrongly believed that such devices would cause unemployment, and the monopolistic guilds feared the increased competition.

In trade, however, the ability of authorities to impede entrepreneurs was more limited. First, in trade across borders one authority could not impose regulations on another. Second, and perhaps just as important, authorities were unable to enforce those regulations they could impose. As an example, Portugal did not have nearly enough ships to preclude smuggling of goods in violation of its attempts to monopolize the spice trade. Governments simply did not possess the wherewithal to monitor interstate commerce sufficiently to effectively impede its growth. Trade was the area that first and most effectively escaped the burden of governmental regulation. It is not surprising that trade became the engine of economic growth.

With the collapse of the feudal system, at least in Western Europe, there opened a power vacuum in that there was no strong central authority to control the rise of the merchant class and the expansion and development of the market system of organizing resources. It is true that King Charles I of Spain became Holy Roman Emperor in 1519. However, the Holy Roman Empire really was organized into hundreds of relatively independent principalities. In addition, Charles spent a good deal of his time fighting wars to unite the Christian world and not as much time dealing with the economic system. In the end, he abdicated the Spanish throne in 1556 without having completed his task of trying to unite the empire. During this period, the economic policies he did employ destroyed the formidable Spanish Empire. The war efforts were supported by confiscatory taxation. Trade was impeded by tariffs that also were used to raise revenue for the war efforts. Thus the empire lost power and authority during this period and eventually slid into total dissolution.

The growth of specialized traders in the Western world could only have occurred with the disappearance of the feudal restrictions on movement, wages and prices, and the expansion of markets. Indeed, those countries that had the fewest

---

[44] For this and other examples see Cameron, op. cit., Ch 5.

trade restrictions were the ones that developed most quickly. In the feudal period, it was the Italian city-states which had the greatest economic development as they escaped the feudal system of resource organization and were the first market economies. During the 1450-1750 period two small countries, England and the Netherlands, became powerful due to their willingness to give free reign to entrepreneurs. The Dutch specialized in international commerce and therefore its government could not afford to restrict the ability of the merchant class to develop markets. The cities that made up the Netherlands followed free trade policies. By the middle of the seventeenth century the Dutch shipping fleet was three times larger than the English fleet and larger than all others combined.[45] This concept of freedom from government regulation was also true of their industrial and agricultural sectors, and the Dutch became leaders in these areas as well.

England eventually became a great power as it followed a policy of political economy that allowed individuals to develop trade and innovations. Parliament realistically lacked the power to control its domestic economy. As a result, "British entrepreneurs enjoyed a degree of freedom and opportunity that was virtually unique in the world."[46]

Many people saw the potential for personal gain and the improvement of trade through the real-life application of comparative advantage. This served as a powerful force for the development of markets. The Western world was in a state where the merchant class was able to take advantage of these potential gains from trade and did so. Those countries that had a political system that either explicitly allowed entrepreneurs to innovate and engage in trade, or were unable to enforce what regulations they did impose, developed into world powers.

In the previous chapter we suggested that the attitudes of the population are important in economic development. People must recognize the importance of individuals to society, and individual people must feel capable of making a real difference in their situation. The attitude of merchants and scientists during this period serves as an example.

We have already seen that industry had a steady improvement that was generally market-driven. Much of the major improvement in technology was in shipping. This should be rather obvious: since shipping was the economic sphere that was most free from interference, it was the area offering the greatest rewards for innovation.

By the late seventeenth century, the scientific method had been developed and was being used for purposes of improving lifestyles. While it was not until the eighteenth or nineteenth century that one can observe the body of scientific knowledge being used systematically on a large scale to promote industrial

---

[45] See Cameron, p 114.

[46] Ibid, p 159.

advancement, the concept of individuals being able to understand their environment and to produce things that would improve their situation began to permeate a greater portion of society during the period following the fifteenth century.

During this time, merchants and those engaged in shipping made the intellectual jump to the belief that society was made up of individuals having certain rights which no government could limit or take away. Contrast the twelfth century peasant—tied to the soil and using agricultural practices based upon tradition—with the Dutch merchant of 1650, outfitting ships, purchasing cargo in one part of the world and delivering it to another, and profiting or losing in the venture. The Dutch merchant will eventually come to believe that the government ought not be able to tell him where he can sail his ships, how much he can sell his products for, and how much he can pay for his products.

This belief in the individual and free trade became particularly strong in the British colonies. Britain had, through legislation such as the Navigation Acts, ostensibly put restrictions on colonial trade. However, until 1763 when King George attempted to pay off the debt from the latest British wars, these taxes, tariffs, and restrictions were laxly enforced, if at all. As a consequence, the colonial merchants and shippers developed a sense of individual freedom that helped lead to the American Revolution and the formation of the United States of America with its constitution of liberty.

In Great Britain, the Scottish moral philosopher Adam Smith put forth the economic justification for the case of individual liberty in his *Wealth of Nations* at the same time that Thomas Jefferson was writing the Declaration of Independence. By the close of the eighteenth century, the stage was set for a major leap in the economic growth of the Western world, commonly known as the Industrial Revolution.

The Industrial Revolution: 1750-1880

From the mid-eighteenth century until the last decades of the nineteenth century, the development of the factory system was the dominant feature of the social structure. Prior to this period, production was in what I like to call the "Geppetto model." Most people have seen or read *Pinocchio*. Recall that Pinocchio's father, Geppetto, was an artisan, a clock maker. He built his clocks in his house, the same place from which he retailed them. He did not go to work in a clock factory and return to his home afterwards; neither were his clocks retailed at Wal-Mart.

Prior to the factory system, most production was carried on by artisans working out of small shops or homes. People who wanted to become artisans first became an apprentice and learned the trade. Apprentices might live with artisans, in their houses or in outbuildings. The factory system led to a fundamental change in the worker-employer relationship. Though the early factories were relatively small, the big difference was that a worker came in and did his job but lived somewhere outside the bounds of the employer.

This period was also a period of great population increase and movement of workers from the countryside into the towns and cities. Although the absolute number of agricultural workers did not decline, the growth in population in the cities surpassed that of the countryside. Part of this was due to the wages paid to workers in the cities. The job opportunities in the cities were greater than those in the countryside.

In this period capitalism began to flower. Individuals risked their assets in order to make or purchase machinery in the hope of producing enough product to reward their risk. In order to produce, the new capitalists hired laborers who were paid more in line with their opportunity cost, since, unlike under the feudal system, they could not be forced to work for someone. People migrated to the cities despite what were deplorable living conditions by today's standards because they believed these conditions were better than those in the countryside. For most, the standard of living began to rise.

One often gets the impression that the advent of the Industrial Revolution and the beginning of a system of mass production characterized by the use of machinery and equipment decreased the standard of living of the workers. Certainly life in the cities was unsanitary and cramped, and it is true that women and children worked long, tedious and difficult hours along with the men. But this was still better than what life would have been like had the population increased and remained in the countryside. Women and children often worked long hours at hard labor on the farms as well, but wages were better in the cities.

It is difficult to make definitive statements about how fast capitalism raised the standard of living. One reason is that data was not as meticulously kept as it is today. Also, the Napoleonic wars disrupted economic development from 1795 to 1815. Nonetheless, it is relatively clear that the standard of living of the laboring classes increased from the beginning of the period. Certainly there were losers when the production system changed. This is true of any change in a dynamic economy. If you were an artisan involved in the textile industry, you would have seen your livelihood endangered by competition from the new textile factories that produced vast quantities of textiles much more cheaply than you could. You would have been forced to change your occupation, or find a particular piece of the industry in which you could specialize.

There are a number of reasons why we have been given the impression that capitalism reduced the standard of living of workers, at least in its formative years. A detailed rebuttal to those who have argued that the standard of living fell, as well as an explanation of why historians have argued that capitalism imposed an early burden on the laboring class, is found in a book edited by Friedrich Hayek entitled *Capitalism and the Historians*.[47] But one explanation is that certain literature of the period reflected the views of those who were on the losing end of change. If we view the last thirty-or-so years of America's economic history from the vantage point of an auto worker in Flint, Michigan, much of it would be a rather bleak story. If we view it from that of a person who writes computer software, it would be a rather bright story. The point is to not put absolute trust in the first thing you hear or read—not even the position taken in this chapter that the Industrial Revolution and the rise of capitalism increased the standard of living of the general laboring class. Consider all things carefully.

Having said that, let us move on to a simple statement that can hardly be refuted: The advent of the factory system changed the entire economic system. If you think about it, Geppetto could probably obtain all the wood he needed to build clocks from nearby. But once Geppetto opened up Geppetto's Clockworks and began producing clocks for Sears and Kmart, he surely would need a number of things that didn't exist while Pinocchio was a mere shaver. Factories require greater amounts of raw materials and a method of transporting the raw materials to the factory. They require a system for distributing the goods once they are produced, since the production will be more than the local market can use. The factory system thus emerged simultaneously with improvements in transportation, raw materials production, wholesaling, and retailing. It also coincided with an increase in agricultural productivity, since factory workers now traded their wages for food that would have to be produced on the farms.

Notice that the dominance of a market economy creates incentives for all these things to happen. No one has to be told by some authority to establish the wholesale trade. Someone will realize that a gain can be made for Geppetto and for him by taking Geppetto's product and dispersing it throughout the country. Geppetto, after all, is still a clock maker at heart. There is no reason to believe he can excel at distributing his product. In the old days, people came into the shop where Geppetto worked, and Pinocchio sold them the clock. Now Pinocchio's friend, Jimminy Cricket, has an incentive to market Geppetto's increased clock production for him. The same will be true for those who see that someone must figure out how to get the wood to Geppetto. There will be a potential benefit both to Geppetto and to the person who organizes and delivers the raw materials.

What else happened as capitalism began to develop? One certainly did not need a system that produced a tremendous amount of goods more cheaply if the target market was the rich. There just weren't very many wealthy people. One could, however, make money by lowering the production costs and increasing the supply of goods that could be used by the masses. The first area where the factory

---

[47] (Chicago: The University of Chicago Press, 1954).

system and capitalism really took off was in the textile industry. This resulted in cheap cloth, so the average person could have more than one shirt. The cloth was washable, and sanitary conditions improved.

As we noticed in an earlier chapter, we can think of the Industrial Revolution as a shift to the right of the supply curve, as shown in Figure 12-1. The factory system and capitalism were the advancement in technology and the method of organizing production that reduced the cost of producing. Recall that as the supply curve shifts to the right, prices fall and output rises.

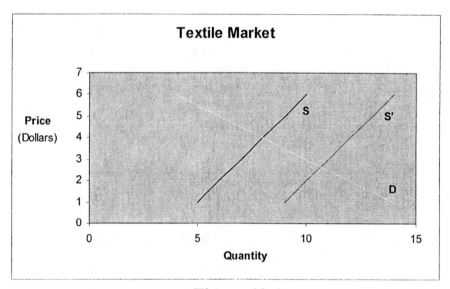

Figure 12-1

This is exactly what happened. The period from 1750-1880 was not one where a large number of new types of goods were produced for the rich, but rather where there was a huge increase in the amount of goods produced for the poor. If one thinks about it, economic advancement in the market systems has the general characteristic that goods become accessible to the poor and middle class that were not even available to the rich but a few decades ago. As Adam Smith notes even at the very beginnings of the Industrial Revolution:

> It may be true, perhaps, that the accommodation of an European prince does not always so much exceed that of an industrious and frugal peasant, as the accommodation of the latter exceeds that of many an African king, that absolute master of the lives and liberties of ten thousand naked savages.[48]

---

[48] Smith, *Wealth of Nations,* op cit., p 24.

Think of how comfortable the average person's living conditions are today compared to those of the richest persons of the seventeenth century.

The economic development that occurred with the general use of markets and the ownership of factories and machinery by individuals was due to the freedom to innovate and produce, as well as the freedom to acquire capital. The lowered cost of production led to short-run economic profits for those who were the first to adopt the new methods. These profits attracted new entrants and increased output and lowered prices. The output of goods in the Western world increased faster than the large increase in population. Sanitary conditions improved as people were able to purchase goods and health amenities. The factory system developed in towns and simply overran the restrictive and monopolistic guild system. The force of the market system was great enough to eventually overthrow the old method of production and the old social order. The rise of the middle class was the inevitable outcome of the rise of capitalism.

Organizational Development: 1880-1914

Looking at our economic environment, we tend to forget that only recently did industry pass agriculture in economic output. The Industrial Revolution, while a major change, did not immediately transform agricultural economies into industrial ones. The factories were small by twentieth-century standards. The need for funds to establish and expand factories could be raised either by partnerships or by the profits from the enterprise itself.

By the late nineteenth century, industrial and organizational developments favored an increase in the size of enterprises. Since there was an advantage to be gained by those who could increase the size of their operations, persons clever enough to determine how to organize their business to raise funds for replacing old factories and building new ones capable of greater output would make a profit. As is always the case where profit can be made from innovating, the innovation took place. In this era, the primary innovation was the method of organizing the firm.

During the Industrial Revolution a business entity came to be distinguished from the individual: Geppetto's clockworks came to be thought of as a separate entity from Geppetto. But it was not until the late nineteenth century that the funds necessary to put into a business became great enough to require the development of the general corporation. When there were sufficient gains to be made from the "invention" of the general corporation, this organizational innovation became inevitable.

Business organizations resembling what we might think of as corporations had been in existence for hundreds of years. The famous Dutch East India Company was established in 1602. But these were business organizations given authority by a specific writ of the government for specific purposes, often for a trade monopoly. The late nineteenth century corporation, on the other hand, was a business organization created to do whatever business it desired and not a privilege granted to an individual by some governmental authority.

Great Britain established some of the earliest general incorporation laws in the early 1800s, but the model for the general corporation was New Jersey's general incorporation statute of 1891. The modern corporation allowed individuals to raise money on a scale sufficient to meet the requirement of a large production facility. One of the important elements of this business organization is marketable stock, which enabled large numbers of unrelated parties to participate in business ownership.

Marketable stock allows a decentralization of business decisions. Instead of a few individuals being able to control the decision whether to undertake an operation or not, anyone can go out and sell shares of stock in the company to a large number of smaller investors. Stock provides a broader access to financial assets than would be the case if you could only get money from people you knew or from a few wealthy people.

Stock also allows individual investors to spread the risk of using their accumulated assets. I can take the money that I have earned as a clock maker and put some of it into a car company like Ford, some of it into a hot chocolate drink manufacturer, like Nestles, and some of it into a software manufacturer like Microsoft. Stock markets are the natural outgrowth of a system whereby investments are made by large numbers of individuals who stand to gain or lose by their decisions.

The Increased Role of Government in the West: 1914-Present

The period of history since 1914 has been one of two world wars and the Great Depression. These social experiences have led to a decline in the belief that individualism and responsibility are the foundation for improved standard of living. Western economies have become substantially regulated, perhaps to the point of strangulation. The size of the government sector has increased enormously since the late nineteenth and early twentieth century. The result is, and will continue to be, a reduction in the incentives to innovate and accumulate capital. This will inevitably lead to a slowing of economic growth, or at least slower economic growth than would occur with an unfettered economy.

As with every historical period, there is no precise date when a transition occurs, nor is the history of any era identical for all parts of the Western world. But there are general trends. We may use the United States as an example. At the beginning of this period, the United States was just beginning to levy an income tax made constitutional by the passage in 1913 of the sixteenth amendment. The Federal Reserve Bank also started in 1913. Today, both of these institutions are a dominant part of the American economy. The federal debt in 1916, just prior to the First World War, stood at $1.2 billion. Even by 1970 the federal debt stood at "only" around $381 billion. Today it is about $5.5 trillion. At the beginning of the 1900s, spending by the United States government as a percentage of national income was around 2.5%. The federal government spends today about one out of every four dollars of national income. The Tax Foundation estimates that that the average person works until May simply to pay their federal, state, and local direct tax burden, and this doesn't count the increased prices consumers face due to the government regulatory burden. Estimates of the reduction in economic output due to federal government regulation exceed $700 billion. The first $500 billion federal budget did not occur until 1979. Today it is in excess of $1.8 trillion.

There are, of course, a number of reasons for the growth of government throughout this period. In fact, a whole literature has developed on the issue, as a subset of the study of public choice. Sometimes it is referred to as the growth of Leviathan, coming from a famous seventeenth century tract by Thomas Hobbes.[49] An interesting hypothesis has been put forth by Professor John Willson of Hillsdale College that the experience of the world wars, especially the Second World War, led people to become accustomed to government intrusion in the economy.[50] This, along with the advent of Keynesian economic theory, which justifies substantial government intervention in the economy, formed the acceptance by the average person that government is the solution to the majority of society's worst social problems. Since democracies reflect the underlying beliefs and general principles of the individuals that make up the country, the recent history has been one of a reinstitution of the combined economic and political sphere. This entails a movement back towards the feudal system of organizing society's resources.

---

[49] Thomas Hobbes, *Leviathan*. Ed. C.B. MacPherson (New York: Penguin Books, 1968).

[50] See John Willson, "World War II: The Great Liberal War," *Imprimus,* May 1992, Hillsdale College Press.

Chapter 13

LESSONS FROM HISTORY

What are we to learn from this brief pass through the last eleven hundred years of Western history? Economic growth has been gradually increasing, and its primary source is innovation: in trade, technology and organization. Innovations overcome the status quo. As ships, factories, and machinery grew in size and number, production likewise expanded. In those periods of history where there has been a union of the political and economic spheres—and governmental authority could squash the opportunity of the individual to improve his or her position in life—there was (and will be) little economic advancement. When individuals have a sphere of life where they are free to accept responsibility for their actions and the consequences of success or failure, economic advancement has occurred.

The development of the market economy occurred over a period of centuries. It was not something that happened on a specific date. As the market economy spread, so did economic development. The development of markets also provided the incentive for the development of those institutions that facilitate markets. This would include, as we pointed out in the last chapter, the corporation and the related body of corporate law. Numerous other institutions have developed in market economies and have assisted in the expansion of markets. These include financial institutions, accounting methods, insurance, the development of a system of taxation rather than servile labor, and a dependable legal system.

Lessons For an Emerging Country

If you were advising a country on how to develop its economy, you could make use of the historical patterns of Western economic growth. The country would need to ensure that its organization of resources was based upon a market system with free trade. There would have to be a separation of the economic and political sphere so that those who were in political power could not restrict the expansion of markets and reduce the incentives of individuals. The legal system would have to be developed to provide strong property rights. A body of corporate law would have to be implemented. The legal system would also have to allow for financial and insurance industries.

Today, a forward-moving country would have the advantage of hundreds of years of Western experience. For example, once it had well-defined property rights and an open market system, then insurance companies would move in. It would not be necessary to reinvent the wheel, so to speak. The institutions that have developed along with markets over the centuries in Western economies would appear as long as the legal means existed for them to do so, since the advantages of these institutions would drive their entry into the system.

A disadvantage that economies which attempt to change quickly from a stagnant, planned economy to a market economy have over economies which moved into a market system gradually is that there will be potential political instability which will threaten the government. This is because resources will have been misdirected by planned economies, and once the system is open to market forces, resources will move to their highest and best use. In order for them to move to their best use, these resources must be released from whatever industry in which they were previously employed. In the case of labor, it means that persons must become unemployed. The greater the misdirection of resources under the planned economy and the longer it has persisted, the larger the number of folks who will enter the unemployment lines. Without a firm belief that a switch to a market economy will truly make things better, people will respond to large amounts of unemployment by political means, creating the uncertainty and instability that keep individuals from investing in the economy, further exacerbating the process. It is, therefore, important that the persons in the country have a firm grasp of market principles and how economic development occurred over time in the advanced countries.

It is also important to keep in mind that those who are in power will normally favor the status quo. This makes sense. If you are already in power, why would you risk losing your position by changing things? Only in one case: where you fear that if you do not change, the threat to your position will be greater. As an example of those in power putting their weight behind a changing environment, some authorities during the period of advancing trade (1450-1750) began to favor the expansion of markets and trade because they found the provision of trade monopolies and trade taxation to be a new source of revenue to fund their wars and expand their power. This aided the development of markets, since the political authority lent its favor and support— and since much of the expansion occurred without the burden of monopoly and taxes because of the inability of the government to effectively police smuggling.

Because there generally exists a bias against change and innovation from those who are in power, it is necessary that the ability to innovate and present new products and methods of production be spread throughout the economy. The Western economies have managed to do this through the market system. Anyone who wishes to invent a new clock has the ability to go to potential investors and try to persuade them to risk putting their money behind the development and marketing of the clock. Geppetto could go to his friends and friends of friends for support. He could go to established commercial banks, issue shares in the new company, or raise the funds in any number of ways. Geppetto does not need the approval of the Department of Commerce to produce his new clock (at least not yet).

The same has been true of Western science. Scientists can find employment in any number of ways. They may work for private firms, such as DuPont, for a nonprofit foundation, for an independent laboratory, for a university, or for any number of government agencies, for example. The growth of Western science has been aided by its structure (or perhaps its lack thereof), namely, a diffusion of authority over the spread of ideas. No authority, such as the church or any governmental ministry, has sole power to decide which ideas will be discussed or developed into a new product. If all new ideas needed the approval of some existing authority, the growth of science would be slow. Look at the difference between scientific advancement during the Middle Ages, when religious and political authorities passed judgment on new ideas, and today when the market passes judgment. The technology of toys is nearing that of the space program, as space aliens battle us in three dimensions with surround-sound. We can imagine where science would be if its every development and advance had always needed approval of the authorities.

Lessons for Western Economies

One of the most important foundations for economic growth is a moral system compatible with private ownership of the means of production (capitalism) and a belief in individual responsibility. The rise of the Protestant work ethic and the writings of Adam Smith are examples of the development of these concepts. Since the beginning of the First World War, we have seen a decline in the belief that individuals are responsible for their actions and that the market system produces results which are morally acceptable. Two World Wars and a Depression provide an opportunity for those who argue the need for government planning and a social ordering. Such people base their arguments upon the feeling that individuals are powerless to improve their situations and are entitled to receive goods and services regardless of their efforts.

Much has been written about this particular world view. Mises, in his 1927 book, *Liberalism*, alerted us to the problems that arise from such opinions.[51] Hayek wrote *The Road to Serfdom* in 1944 in an attempt to point out the adverse consequences of the trend towards greater government intervention in the social and economic spheres. Another Nobel Prize-winning economist, Milton Friedman, wrote *Capitalism and Freedom* in 1962 as a further warning.[52] In the 1970s he followed this with *Free to Choose*.[53] The gist of these works is that if we move

---

[51]See *Liberalism in the Classical Tradition*, 3rd edition (Irvington-on-Hudson: Foundation for Economic Education, 1985). The first edition was published in 1927.

[52] *Capitalism and Freedom* (Chicago: University of Chicago Press, 1962).

[53] Milton and Rose Friedman, *Free to Choose* (New York: Harcourt Brace Jovanovich, 1979)

back to an existence where the authorities are able to determine for whom we may work and under what conditions, as well as what we may produce and how, and if people are taught that they are not capable of directing their lives and personally improving their station, and that it is the existing authority that possesses the solutions to social problems—not the people—then we will have done nothing but tragically reverted to the very beginning of Western economic development. We will have returned to square one. Do not pass go, and do not collect two hundred dollars.

We are then right back to a situation where the incentives to innovate have seriously declined, and the result is slower economic growth than would otherwise have been the case. But, as Richard Weaver points out, ideas have consequences.[54] The early warnings of Mises, Hayek, and Friedman have not generally affected the actions of those who run the government. While laying the groundwork for many freemarketers to follow, the writings of free market advocates have made precious little dent in the conception of the average person concerning how the world works—until recently.[55] We may yet be reaching a turning point.

Today we have numerous scholarly books and articles arguing what Bastiat was already saying one hundred and fifty years ago, that government intervention in the market will lead to bigger government and an allocation of resources based on political power rather than efficiency in use and pleasing of consumers. Rush Limbaugh, a free market advocate, now attracts over 15 million radio listeners and his two books have been best sellers. At the national level, free market institutions, such as the CATO Institute, the Manhattan Institute, the Institute for Humane Studies, the Heritage Foundation, the Foundation for Economic Education, and the Intercollegiate Studies Institute, have sprung up and are growing in size and number. Local and regional policy institutes, such as the Mackinac Center in Michigan, and the Heartland Institute in Illinois have become influential in state and regional policy debates.

Our government and its policies do not yet reflect the return of the market as a means of ordering society. The majority of Americans continue to believe in an interventionist state where government interferes in the social ordering in some form of mixed economy. However, people are beginning to realize that something is basically wrong. By using common sense, questioning the presentations of the media, and looking for what Bastiat calls "the unseen," each of us can pretty well figure out what is really happening and make a reasoned presentation to friends and relatives.

---

[54] See his extraordinary book, *Ideas Have Consequences* (Chicago: University of Chicago Press, 1984, originally published in 1948..

[55] For a discussion of why this might be the case, see Friedrich Hayek, "The intellectuals and Socialism," *The University of Chicago Law Review,* Vol. 16, No. 3, Spring 1949.

Chapter 14

THE ROLE OF GOVERNMENT AND MACROECONOMIC THEORY

Basic Definitions

We have spent the last three chapters discussing progress and economic growth, but we have not yet sought precise definitions. We have sort of understood progress and economic growth as Justice Potter Stewart defines pornography: "I'll know it when I see it." But we can imagine how we might go about measuring economic product.

One way might be to list all the goods and services produced and their amounts. While this may be conceptually possible, it would not at all be feasible. In fact, it may not even be conceptually possible. For example, how many units of education were produced in the United States last year? We do not have a clear idea how to measure units of education. Hours of instruction might do, but one might think of hours of instruction as an input into producing the service of increased knowledge. You can easily think of many problems in trying to measure many different services.

An obvious alternative is to measure the dollar value of goods and services. This too has some problems, but it is the option most often used. The most common measurement is called Gross Domestic Product.

Just as an aside, think of how often you have heard one of those talking heads on network national news tell you that GDP went up by some percent or other last quarter. This is usually big television news and attracts print coverage as well. Now think of how many people listening to the news program, including yourself, could define GDP. How many of the talking heads who are telling you about the change in GDP could define it?

Presuming that none of you rushed out to look up GDP in an economics book the last time one of these stories appeared on television, we shall proceed.

Gross Domestic Product is the dollar value of all final goods and services produced in the economy in a given time period, usually in one year. Now what do we mean by a final good? We mean a good that is either purchased by an end consumer, like a video game, or a capital good that is purchased by a producer, like a stamping mold. We only count final goods and services because we don't want to count things more than once as they move through the production process.

For example, suppose we produced three tons of steel in the last year, and this steel was then made into two cars. At the end of the year all we have are the two cars. The steel has been used up in the production of the cars. If we were to count the steel and the cars in GDP, then it would look like the economy had produced more than it actually had.

One way to determine GDP for the U.S. economy for last year would be to add up the value of all the final goods and services. You would count up the value of all the cars sold, all the compact disc players, all the drill presses, etc. Now you would have to be careful that if the car was sold with a compact disc player in it, you didn't count the player twice, once when it was sold to the auto company and once when the auto company sold the car. Basically you would be careful to exclude what are called intermediate goods, those goods which are transformed in the production process into other goods.

Another way to arrive at the same number is to determine what the "value added" is at each stage of production. "Value added" is what each firm adds to the value of the product as the product moves along in the production process. In the simplest terms, this would be the firm's sales minus what it purchased from other firms. The standard example of determining value added is the production of bread.

Suppose a farmer begins the year with some seed left over from last year, a tractor, and some diesel fuel. The farmer sows his seed and harvests $200 worth of wheat. Since the farmer didn't purchase anything from anyone else that year, the farmer's value added would be $200. The farmer then sells the wheat to the miller. The miller grinds the wheat up into flour, then sells the flour to the bakery for $300. The miller's value added is the $300 sale to the bakery minus the $200 spent on the wheat, or $100. The bakery then takes the flour and turns it into bread. It sells the bread for $450 to the retail grocer. The bakery's value added would be $450 (its sales) minus its purchases of the flour of $300, or $150. Finally, the grocer sells the bread for $500 to its customers. The grocer's value added is $500 (its sales) minus $450 (its purchases from other firms), or $50. At the end of the year, the economy will have produced $500 worth of bread, that is the value of the final good. If we add up the amount of value added by each producer along the way, we should get the total value of the bread, or $500. Adding up the value added of the farmer, miller, baker and grocer we get $200+$100+$150+$50, which equals $500, the value of the bread.

Computation of "Value Added"			
	Sales	Purchases	Value Added
Farmer	$200	$0	$200
Miller	$300	$200	$100
Bakery	$450	$300	$150
Grocer	$500	$450	$50
Total			$500

Table 14-1

Most European countries, as well as a number of other countries, use value added as the basis for their taxation of business. The United States, on the other hand, uses a corporate income tax as its primary method of taxing business activity both at the federal and the state level.[56] Lately there has been public debate about instituting a value added tax at the federal level. This would be a tax that each business would have to pay on its value added. As you can see from our example, the base for a value added tax is the same as the base for a sales tax. That is, in our example, we could either have imposed the tax on the final sale of bread or imposed the tax on the value added at each stage. In either case, the base of the tax would be $500. While we need not go into detail on the pros and cons of a value added tax and a comparison to a corporate income tax, you will at least be one step ahead of most Americans when it comes to deciding whether your government is doing the right thing by imposing or not imposing a value added tax. Most folks won't have the vaguest idea of what a value added tax is, including many of the folks who could possibly be voting on the issue.

Another term often used in the media and at cocktail parties, is "inflation." Inflation may also be like pornography, but the headline story will be pretty specific. For example, we might read that inflation rose by 1.2% last month, or 3.3% over the last year. What do we mean by inflation as a concept, and how do we measure it?

Inflation is a decline in the value of money. This occurs when the price of all goods taken as a group rise. Inflation is not when the prices of some goods go up and the prices of some goods go down. This is what we have already analyzed as a change in relative prices. People often confuse relative price changes with inflation. When you can buy less of all goods with the same amount of money, then you have inflation.

Given this definition of inflation, it should be obvious that only one thing can cause inflation: an increase in the amount of money relative to goods in the economy. It is not caused by union requests for higher wages, or by increases in the price of oil, or by the existence of monopolies. All these things may change relative prices, but they cannot cause a general price increase unless they are accompanied by a rise in the amount of money in circulation. Later on we will see that in today's economies, it is the government that controls, or attempts to control, the amount of money. Thus, inflation can only be created by government.

How do we measure inflation? There are various indices that are used to measure inflation, but the most common one is the Consumer Price Index, or CPI. It is to this that the media refers when the headline in the paper says, "last month's inflation was 3.4% on an annual basis." Millions of people will read this headline,

---

[56] Michigan uses a value added tax, called the Single Business Tax, for its business activity. It is the only state using a value added tax, although Texas and Florida are discussing the possibility of adopting one.

or hear it on the nightly news. Yet, as with GDP, few will be able to answer Bullwinkle's question, "What does this mean?"

The consumer price index is a measure of the cost of a basket of goods compared to the cost for that same basket of goods in an earlier period. The Bureau of Labor Statistics (BLS) goes out and surveys folks to find out what they generally buy. They then do a little shopping and get the prices of these goods and figure out what it costs to buy this "typical" market basket. The next month they go out and see how much it costs to buy this same market basket. By comparing the change in costs, they get a measure of inflation. If the cost went down by one-twelfth of a percent, then (forgetting about compounding) on an annual basis you have a 1% deflation rate. If the cost went up by one-twelfth of one percent, then on an annual basis you would have an inflation rate of 1%.

The CPI itself is a number that is based on a scale of one hundred. The BLS picks a date to do its survey of the typical market basket. The cost of the market basket is indexed to one hundred. One way of thinking about this is to say at that date, the cost of the market basket is 100% of the original market basket. If you looked at the cost of the same market basket one year later, and it was 5% higher, then the consumer price index would read 105, or 105% of the original cost. Thus, if the CPI is 286, then this means that buying the same market basket of goods today costs 286% of its original cost.

As with any measure of inflation, there are some problems with this. First, the typical market basket has to change over time. People won't be buying the same things in 2005 that they were buying in 1955. The BLS does go out and change the market basket every few years. Its statisticians then try to make the CPI consistent over the entire period. Obviously, however, the measure won't be as good as it would have been in the twelfth century when people bought the same stuff year after year for decades.

A second problem is trying to account for improvements or changes in goods. A 1953 Pontiac, although an automobile, is not be exactly the same vehicle as a 2003 Pontiac. A 1953 television is not quite the same product as a 2003 television. Thus, part of what you are measuring in the CPI is improvement in the quality of the product.

Some economists argue that the concept of the CPI is rather ridiculous anyway. Each of us has our own market basket of goods that we buy, and we have a pretty good idea of what is happening to it. We don't need the government to give us a number to tell us what is happening to prices. While this type of argument may be true, nonetheless, there is a market demand for measures like the CPI from policy makers, and now the from news media, since they believe that policy makers alter government policy based upon these measures.

Basic Macroeconomic Theory: The Keynesian Model

Macroeconomic theory is used to study the behavior of what we can call economic aggregates: the behavior of the economy as a whole. Items falling under the study of macroeconomics include the total amount of output produced in an economy (GDP), changes in the aggregate price level (inflation), and equilibrium conditions in the overall labor market (unemployment). Macroeconomics emphasizes the role of government in affecting these things through its taxation and spending policies and its control (or lack of control) of the money supply.

Entire textbooks are written on macroeconomics, as well as hundreds of articles in academic journals. Some economists specialize in macroeconomics and different subtopics within the field of macroeconomics. The intent here is to provide you with enough of the subject so you can comprehend the basic arguments, understand why politicians say they are doing what they are doing (or are going to do), make judgments about your government's actions, and ask a question or two of those who would provide an argument for a given government policy.

One thing to keep in mind is something that one of my professors in graduate school used to always ask whenever a Ph.D. student would present a paper in our graduate seminar. Often these papers were done to show off the student's mathematical skill and sense of the arcane. After the student would go through some long and detailed mathematical model to reach some conclusion, Professor Rolph would sit back and say, "Now tell me a story about why that is true." Whenever you are presented a complicated mathematical model that reaches a conclusion that doesn't appeal to you, ask the person doing the explaining to tell you a simple story about why that is true. This is because most models will reach results that are mathematically consistent with their assumptions. It is usually the assumptions that cause the problem.

The basic macroeconomic model owes its existence to Lord John Maynard Keynes. He developed his theory in response to the circumstances of the Great Depression of the 1930's. Until the publication of his book, *The General Theory of Employment, Interest, and Money*, the dominant belief was that the economy would reach equilibrium at full employment after any shocks push it out of its original equilibrium.[57] There could not be long periods of excess supply of labor, since wages would decline until the market cleared. As unemployment dragged on for years during the Great Depression, the classical economists' argument for how the economy behaves lost its firm foundation. Keynes' book posited that the economy could reach equilibrium at a spot where unemployment remained, and

---

[57] *The General Theory of Employment, Interest, and Money* (Amherst, New York: Prometheus, 1997) was first published in 1936.

that in fact this was what was happening in 1936. Because the Keynesian explanation for what was happening appeared to be more consistent with the world situation, it began to be accepted. Within thirty years the theory of Keynes, at least as interpreted by his followers, had become macroeconomic theory. Since *The General Theory* is one of those classic books that no one has read but everyone is familiar with, this chapter will examine Keynesian theory from the way that it is usually depicted in macroeconomics textbooks.

The basic principle of macroeconomic theory is aggregation. You must first imagine that it makes sense to conceive that you can take the numerous goods and services that exist or might exist in the economy and clump them all together into one good and assign a unit of measurement to it. You then can think of demand for this aggregated good and supply of this good. Once you are comfortable with this basic concept, then macroeconomics begins to make sense. The basic model turns on the idea of aggregate demand and aggregate supply.

If you are having trouble conceiving of this aggregate product, you are not alone. How is aggregate demand affected by a change in consumer demand from shoes to shirts? How is aggregate supply affected by cessation of production of Pontiac Firebirds and increased milk production? Many economists of the Austrian School of thought wonder if any of this makes sense. The Austrian approach is more interested in the behavior of individual markets and the interactions across markets. In any event, think of the total production of the economy as one good that can be assigned units of amount and a price.

If you think of the price of this aggregated good as being the Consumer Price Index, then you are ready to think of an aggregate demand curve and an aggregate supply curve. Using the same reasoning that we did for the demand and supply of individual products in our earlier chapters, we would expect the demand curve for production as a whole to slope down. At higher prices, people will demand less and as the prices fall they will demand more. Suppliers will supply less goods on the whole when prices are low and will supply more as prices rise. We can picture this in Figure 14-1, where AD is aggregate demand and AS is aggregate supply.[58]

---

[58] There are much more complicated ways of generating a downward sloping aggregate demand curve. The same is true of the upward sloping aggregate supply curve. These are detailed in any intermediate macroeconomics text. For our purposes, we can simply assume a downward sloping aggregate demand curve and an upward sloping aggregate supply curve.

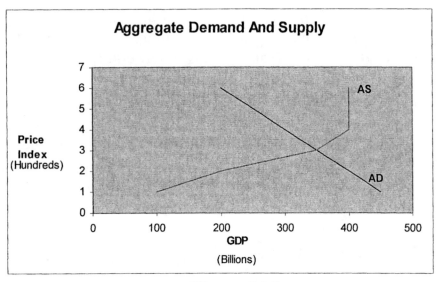

Figure 14-1

Notice what happens to our aggregate supply curve, AS. At some level of output, about $400 billion in Figure 14-1, the curve becomes vertical. This expresses the hypothesis that there is some quantity of output where all the nation's resources, or at least all of its labor resources, are fully employed. No more output will be produced even if prices continue to rise. We will call this full employment output.

Equilibrium for the entire economy comes at about $350 billion in Figure 14-1, where the quantity demanded for all goods just equals the quantity supplied for all goods, or where AD intersects AS. Again transferring the same arguments that we used in earlier chapters, at this equilibrium quantity and price there will be no incentive for producers to produce more or less or for prices to change. The economy will be at rest.

The key to all of this is that there is nothing in this model that ensures that the equilibrium level of output will be the same as the output level which corresponds to full employment. In terms of the diagram, in general, the output level where aggregate demand intersects aggregate supply will not be at the same output level as that which represents full employment. This is basically Keynes' explanation for how unemployment could have existed for several years during the Great Depression. The economy had come to its equilibrium GDP at a level of output that was not sufficient to employ everyone.

The obvious question is: "How can we get the economy to come to an equilibrium at an output which is equal to full employment?" The answer that was most often used over a forty-year period or so, from about 1940 to about 1980, was to shift the aggregate demand curve. If we can get people to demand more of the total product at every level of prices, we can get an increase in output sufficient to

117

reach full employment. This is similar to our noting that if you advertise successfully you can get people to want to buy more of your product at every price, thus shifting demand to the right, and getting a new equilibrium at a higher level of output and a higher price. The same idea holds here.

In Figure 14-2 we see that the aggregate demand curve has shifted from AD to AD', thus resulting in a new equilibrium where the equilibrium level of output is the same as the full employment output. If we can shift the aggregate demand curve, then we can get the economy out of its state of unemployment. Although we get an increase in the consumer price index, from about 275 to about 375, we get a higher level of output and eliminate the unemployment.

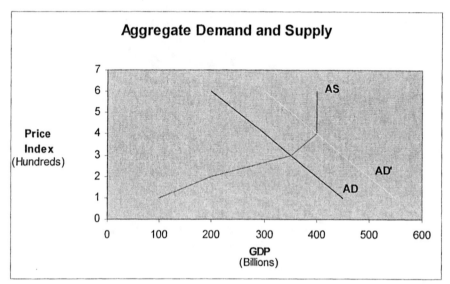

Figure 14-2

The next question is: "How do we shift the aggregate demand curve?" In order to answer this question, we break down the components of aggregate demand, and then look at how we can affect each of the components. In the simplest model, where we ignore exports and imports, we can think of dividing total demand for all goods into the demand for consumer goods, the demand for investment goods, and the demand for government goods. Then we can see how we can affect the demand for each of these types of goods.

Consumer goods are goods that consumers purchase for their final enjoyment. These would include television sets, compact disc players, hula hoops, as well as services such as car repair, house painting, and lawn mowing. This would not include intermediate goods, or goods which are used to produce other goods. Now, how can we affect the demand for consumer goods?

From a public official's point of view, we could advertise, just as businesses advertise. But let us assume that businesses are already advertising at the amount which each of them feels is the correct amount. Income, therefore, is the answer. We have already noted that income affects people's demands for goods and services. The government can most directly affect people's income through taxes. That is because what people use to purchase goods and services is their income after the government has taken its taxes. Raising people's taxes reduces their spending income, generally called disposable income, while reducing taxes increases their disposable income. We would expect, then, that reducing taxes would shift the aggregate demand curve to the right, and as such would be one policy tool that governments can use to reduce unemployment. Of course, raising taxes will shift the aggregate demand curve to the left, reducing output and increasing unemployment, unless the economy is in the range of the aggregate supply curve where the curve is vertical.

The 1964 tax reduction proposed by President Kennedy and implemented by President Johnson after Kennedy's assassination was an attempt to move the economy out of a recession. It is often cited as a successful application of Keynesian theory to solving the problem of unemployment. When taxes were reduced, people demanded more goods, the demand curve shifted to the right, output increased, and prices did as well. The President Reagan tax cuts of 1981 might be viewed by some as an application of the Keynesian model where a substantial tax cut resulted in increased output and reduced unemployment.

Another component of aggregate demand is investment demand. This is the demand for capital goods, that is, machinery and equipment, buildings, and inventories. These are essentially goods that are used to produce another good. There is a large body of literature on what affects the demand for goods like these. In its simplest terms, which is all we need to understand the general idea of what is going on, the interest rate is at least one determinant of investment demand. The higher the interest rate, the lower the demand for investment, and the lower the interest rate, the higher the demand for investment.

A simple way of explaining this is to think of what must induce you to buy a machine. First, suppose you must borrow money to buy the machine. If so, then you will have to get enough added production from the machine to pay for the cost of the loan. This includes the interest payments you must make for borrowing the money. Suppose the machine costs $100 and you borrow the $100 for ten years at 10%. Then the added product from the machine must generate enough money for you to pay back the $100 plus all the interest payments you make. If the interest were at 2%, then the machine would have to generate less product to make it worth your while to buy the machine, since the interest payments would be smaller. Thus, the lower the interest rate, the better chance there is that you will find it worth your while to buy the machine.[59] Lower interest rates result in greater investment demand.

Now suppose that you are going to purchase the machine from company earnings instead of borrowing. If you had taken the money you intended to spend on the machine and put it in a bank, or bought a certificate of deposit, or shares in a mutual fund, or whatever, you would have earned the going market interest rate. This is your opportunity cost of buying the machine. The higher the interest rate, the greater the opportunity cost of buying the machine, and the fewer machines that will be purchased. Thus, higher interest rates result in lower demand for investment goods and lower interest rates result in higher investment demand. Thus, a second way the government could move the economy out of a recession would be to lower interest rates (assume for now that it can). This would increase investment demand, which would increase aggregate demand, and thus increase equilibrium GDP.

The third component of aggregate demand is the demand for government goods. By government goods, we mean goods and services that are demanded by governments. Examples would be roads, anti-aircraft weapons, office buildings, and bridges. Government spending which represents transfers of income from one person to another, such as when I pay Social Security taxes and the government gives that money to your grandmother in the form of a Social Security check, are not part of government demand. This is because your grandmother's Social Security check ends up in her consumer demand. If we counted government spending on Social Security in aggregate demand, it would be counted twice. When your grandmother bought her new microwave with her social security check, it was counted as consumer demand.

Increases in government demand also increase aggregate demand, and thus increase equilibrium GDP. This is the basic reasoning behind the theory that war spending by government will move an economy out of a recession or depression. By adding to government demand, it adds to aggregate demand, thus moving the equilibrium GDP to full employment GDP.

We have just looked at three ways of shifting aggregate demand: (1) changing taxes; (2) changing interest rates; and (3) changing government demand. The first and third of these, taxes and government spending, are known as fiscal policy. Interest rates are changed through the government changing the money supply, and thus is known as monetary policy. When you hear that government fiscal policy is loose, it means that the government is either lowering taxes, increasing government spending, or a combination of the two. When you hear that

---

[59] Just as there is diminishing marginal utility from buying more of a good, there is diminishing marginal product from adding more machines after a certain point. This means that when interest rates get lower, and you have to get less of a product in order to make them pay for themselves, you can add machines that have less marginal product. This is just another way of noticing that the demand for investment will go up as interest rates go down.

monetary policy is loose, it means that government is reducing interest rates through increasing the money supply. We will discuss monetary policy more in the next chapter.

Fiscal Policy: Does it Work?

There is a mountain of literature on whether or not fiscal policy actually works. After the apparent triumph of Keynesian fiscal policy with the Kennedy-Johnson tax cut, which was followed by the then-longest peacetime expansion in U.S. history, it appeared that Keynesian theory had won the day. But even then, economists such as Friedrich Hayek, Henry Hazlitt, and Milton Friedman were arguing that fiscal policy was not effective and was not really the reason for the expansion. By the late 1970's, with the inflation and recession of the Jimmy Carter administration, the Keynesians were somewhat in retreat. For example, a new school of thought, which still relies on the basic Keynesian model, called rational expectations, came to the conclusion that both monetary and fiscal policy will not work in the long run. Friedman's monetarist views, that fiscal policy doesn't work and that monetary policy ought to consist of stabilizing the money supply, had also reached high ground.

Some of President Reagan's key advisors were called supply-siders because they felt that it was not possible to reach equilibrium at full employment through trying to shift the aggregate demand curve, or at least this was an ineffective way of increasing GDP. They thought instead that the government ought to concentrate on shifting the supply curve. The Reagan tax cut was seen not as an attempt to shift aggregate demand, but as an attempt to increase the reward for producing, by reducing taxes on income, and thus shifting the supply curve out. In Figure 14-3 we can see that shifting the supply curve out will increase equilibrium GDP and lower prices.

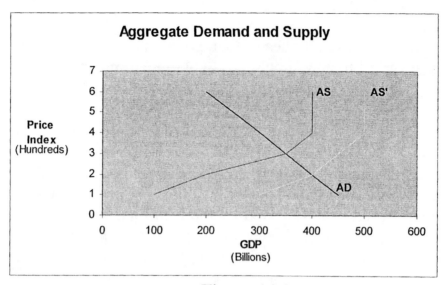

Figure 14-3

In any event, for those who will move on to further study economics, an array of writings on the effectiveness of fiscal (and monetary) policy awaits you. Some of it is tedious, but a good deal of it is interesting.

Keynesian Economics and the Role of Government

Keynes envisioned that the government's fiscal and monetary policy would be run by economists who would increase spending and reduce taxes when the economy was at equilibrium at less than full employment. They would also increase taxes and reduce spending when the economy was already at full employment and aggregate demand kept increasing. Notice in this model, once you are at full-employment GDP, increases in demand just bid up the general price level, in other words, cause inflation.

Nobel Laureate James Buchanan and his colleague Richard Wagner point out one problem with the Keynesian model in some detail in their book *Democracy in Deficit: The Political Legacy of Lord Keynes*.[60] They note that, at least in the U.S., the Congress controls spending and taxes, and that congressmen are elected through the democratic process. If a congressman promises that he will reduce your taxes and still get that road repaved in your neighborhood, then an opponent who says that if you want your road paved you will have to pay more taxes doesn't stand a chance. Thus, in a democracy, there is a natural tendency to increase spending and increase the federal debt. The Keynesian model which says that it is the role of government to ensure full employment and that it is good policy to increase spending and decrease taxes, results in federal deficits on a regular basis.

---

[60] *Democracy in Deficit: The Political Legacy of Lord Keynes* (New York: Academic Press, 1977)

The persistent federal deficits that occurred until quite recently in the United States began with the establishment of the Keynesian revolution in the political process. From the beginning of the Kennedy administration in 1961 until 1998 there was only one year, 1969, when the federal government did not run a deficit.

The idea that federal deficits were a problem began to take hold with the strong showing of Ross Perot in the 1992 presidential election. A major theme of his candidacy was that federal deficits were bad for the economy. He, in effect, reinstated the belief that we should seek a balanced federal budget. This has led us to a point where the federal budget is in surplus.

There is another body of literature on whether deficits matter and why they matter if they do. In any event, it is relatively clear that the government ran large and continuing deficits for decades at least in part because of the Keynesian revolution .

One point I would like to make about the role of government and Keynesian economics is that it starts with the assumption that the proper role of government is to stabilize the economy, nearly to the exclusion of all other discussion. In the basic Keynesian model, all government spending increases GDP. There is no discussion, such as we saw in Bastiat, about whether spending on agricultural research, for example, falls within the proper theory of the role of government in society. Since any government spending increases GDP, and since the role of government is to maintain the economy at full employment, nearly all government spending becomes justified.

Notice in particular that it doesn't matter what government spends your money on. If the government hires you to dig holes and fill them up again, then government spending has increased. This increases aggregate demand, and this increases GDP. It is this feature of the model that leads to conclusions like one that you may have heard: World War II saved us from the Great Depression. Somehow, by hiring people to make airplanes and taking them over to Europe and blowing them up, our economy became better off. When faced with such a proposition, that wars are good for the economy because they increase aggregate demand, I suggest that you follow that professor of mine and ask the person to tell you a story about why that is true. Have them tell you a story about why having people build tanks and blow them up, and having people not produce goods for four years but instead wander through deserts and European fields and Pacific jungles shooting at other people, and having people live in tents and having bureaucrats ration goods, could possibly have resulted in turning the economy around. Talk to someone who was alive then about living standards during World War II. Thousands of people who were in military service spent nights sleeping outside or in tents or on ships. Goods were rationed. It was difficult to obtain consumer goods such as nylon stockings and gasoline. Yet as measured, GDP was going up.

Keynesian economics represents a much broader view of the role of government than a Bastiat-Mises-Hayek train of thought. A Keynesian does not even discuss whether it is the proper role of government to be engaged in taking from some people to provide others with a free college education. Increased government spending on higher education, or on anything for that matter, will increase aggregate demand and thus yield a higher GDP, and that is the end of it. Such a theory results in an interventionist policy that Mises says can only lead to socialism. It is why he had such nasty things to say about Keynes in some of his writings. It is what Hayek warned about in *The Road to Serfdom* and the *Constitution of Liberty*.

Most of the discussion in opposition to Keynesian policy prescriptions involves whether Keynesian policy prescriptions actually work to increase GDP. But one interesting discussion topic is how Keynesian policy fits into the concept of a free society. When you are engaged in further study of the matter, or just in conversation with your neighbor, don't stop at whether policy prescriptions for taxing and spending work. Ask the question about how these prescriptions fit into our view of how a free society should be organized.

Chapter 15

MONEY AND THE ROLE OF GOVERNMENT

In the last chapter we mentioned monetary policy and said it is one tool that government can use to attempt to affect aggregate demand. More specifically, monetary policy refers to government's ability to affect the money supply to pursue its goal of improving the economy. As with fiscal policy, there is considerable debate about whether monetary policy is a useful tool for government and little debate about the proper role of government in the market for money.

What is Money?

Let's define "money." Most macroeconomics texts provide a formal definition of money as currency in the hands of the public and demand deposits. This is normally labeled M1. In other words, M1 is paper money and coins that people have in their pockets and checking accounts. (The latter are called demand deposits by economists in order to confuse you.) There are different levels of Ms. M2 includes the things in M1, plus certain savings-type accounts. One can continue through the Ms, adding things that are further removed from what you actually use in the store to buy something. The particular measure of money an economist might use to define money depends upon what is being researched. When predicting next month's interest rates it may be that M1 is a better explanation than M2. On the other hand, it may be that guessing next quarter's GDP will require use of M2. One might use M3 to explain variations in the value of the dollar against foreign currencies. However, when you see in the newspaper that the money supply increased by 3% last quarter, then it usually means M1. If it says the broadly defined money supply, it usually means M2. M3 and higher Ms are usually used only by economists in writing technical articles.

Aside from any formal definitions, we can think of what money is by simply using our common sense: money is whatever good we use to facilitate exchange. Thinking of money this way is probably best, since doing so provides insight as to whether we need government in order to have money.

In an economy that is based on specialization and exchange there has to be a way for one person to trade their goods or services with a person who has something the first person desires. For example, if I want to buy a shirt, in a barter system I would have to find someone who has a shirt in the style I want and the size I need who is willing to trade it for an economics lecture. Now I know that you're thinking, who wouldn't want to trade whatever they have for an economics lecture? Even so, it would still be difficult. Money is clearly the way to get around this problem. I trade economics lectures to Hillsdale College for dollars. I then trade these dollars to the person who owns the clothing store for the shirt. This system works much better.

Money, then, is really a medium of exchange. Once we see this, other points of interest come to mind. An obvious one is that lots of different goods can serve as money. Baseball cards could serve as money if people were willing to accept them in exchange. In fact, over the centuries many different goods have served as money, even in the United States, where tobacco served as money for a period of time.[61]

A second point: we don't really need government to have money. Since there are obvious advantages to inventing money, something or other would have developed as markets grew more sophisticated. Whenever there are enormous gains to be made from devising something, it will be devised. The advantage of a system of exchange based upon money over a system of barter is obvious. Money necessarily would have come into use without the need of a governmental authority to provide it.[62]

To reinforce this point, suppose that tomorrow the government of the United States says it is recalling all United States dollars, and that there will be no more government money. Do you think that we would all go back to the barter system? Of course not, banks, insurance companies, and new firms would all offer notes that we could use as money. As long as people would accept them in exchange for other goods, then these new notes would make up the money supply.

Indeed, for lengthy periods of our country's history, state-chartered banks issued currency. In 1913 the Federal Reserve Act resulted in the federal monopolization of currency. Since then the value of the dollar has declined until it is worth only 10% of its 1913 value.

How Do Banks Create Money?

The first paper money was probably receipts for gold deposited with goldsmiths. Before banks, people would take their gold to a goldsmith for safekeeping. The goldsmith would issue a warehouse receipt for the gold. After awhile, people would just exchange the receipts rather than the gold. Suppose you had 3 ounces of gold at Harry's Goldsmith Shop. You then buy my cottage for the 3 ounces of gold. You could go to Harry's, get the gold, give it to me, and then I could deposit it back with Harry. Or, you could just give me the receipt for the gold. In this way, the gold warehouse receipts began to be money, since they were accepted in exchange for goods.

---

[61] One book containing a history of what has served as money is *Money: Whence it Came, Where it Went*, by John Kenneth Galbraith, (De Plaines, Ill.: Bantam Books, 1976).

[62] For a discussion of the beginnings of money based upon this general idea, see Ludwig von Mises, *The Theory of Money and Credit* (New Haven: Yale University Press, 1953), originally written in 1912 as *Theorie des Geldes und der Umlaufsmittel*.

It probably didn't take goldsmiths too long to figure out that not everybody came back to their warehouse for their gold at the same time. If they had 100 ounces of gold in their warehouse, on any given day they might have to give up 3 ounces of gold. So, why not lend out some of this gold to other folks? A merchant might come in to borrow 10 ounces of gold to purchase some silk from the Chinese, and then pay the 10 ounces back when he sold the silk to the Italians. The goldsmith could easily lend out the 10 ounces, charge 1 ounce of gold for interest and make a tidy profit. As long as all the goldsmith's customers didn't show up at the same time to get their gold, he was covered and this system worked.

This is how your banks operate today. If you put $1000 in your favorite bank, only a fraction will stay at the bank. The bank will then lend the rest of it to someone else. This works as long as you don't have a lot of people wanting to get their money from the bank at the same time. When a lot of people come looking for their money it is called "a run on the bank." In 1933, twenty years after the Federal Reserve system began operating, runs on our nation's banks led to a financial panic.

Before we go any further, let's take a look at how the system works. Let's presume that there is only one bank, FDR Trust. This will make it easier to follow what is happening, but the result is exactly the same if there are thousands of banks. You find $100 cash in your running shorts and decide to deposit it in your checking account at FDR Trust. FDR Trust takes your $100 and opens a checking account for you for $100. The system thus begins with FDR Trust having $100 in liabilities, your checking account, and $100 in assets, the $100 cash you deposited. That would be the end of it, except for the fact that we have fractional reserve banking. Just like the goldsmith, FDR Trust needs to keep only a fraction of that $100 in reserve. It may loan out the rest, if it so wishes. The reserve requirement is set by the Federal Reserve. It infrequently changes the requirement. At the time of this writing the requirement is around 10%. In order to make the numbers easy to work with, let's presume the reserve requirement is 20%. This means that if FDR Trust has $100 in checking accounts, it must keep $20 in reserve in its vaults in case someone wants their money.

At this point, FDR Trust has $80 in excess reserves. It need only keep the $20, that is, 20% of the $100 it has outstanding in checking accounts. Suppose Mary comes in and wants to borrow $80. FDR Trust can charge Mary 8% interest and make a little money on your $100, so it loans Mary the $80. It does this by creating a checking account for Mary at FDR Trust. Now there are $180 worth of checking accounts as liabilities of the bank, and the bank has $180 in assets: the $100 you put in and the $80 loan to Mary. But notice that there is now $180 in money in the economy, because checking accounts are counted as part of the money supply.

Things don't end here, however. FDR Trust has $180 in checking accounts, but it has $100 in reserve: the cash you brought in is still there. In order to support $180 in checking accounts, FDR Trust need only keep 20% of $180, or $36, on reserve. This means that FDR has $64 in excess reserves. So Tom comes in and wants to borrow $64. FDR Trust creates a checking account for Tom for $64 and Tom signs the loan agreement. Now there is $180 plus $64, or $244, in checking accounts. The money supply has more than doubled since we began our story. But FDR Trust still has excess reserves. It has $244 in checking accounts, so need only keep 20%, or $48.80, in reserves. It may still loan out more money.

How long can this continue? Well, if you remember anything about sums of infinite series, you will see that the final money supply can get as large as one divided by the reserve requirement times the original injection of money. In this case, one divided by 20% is the same as one divided by 1/5. This is equal to 5. Multiplying the $100 you found in your running shorts by 5, results in a money supply of $500. Thus your original $100 has been transformed into $500 of checking accounts.

There are some things to notice here. First, it doesn't matter that we used one bank, since all banks are part of this fractional reserve system. If Mary had taken the $80 loan and put it in her bank, then her bank would have $80 in new reserves and $80 in new checking accounts, so it would have had the $64 in excess reserves. As long as everyone's money eventually ends up in a bank, the expansion continues.

Second, the amount of the expansion depends upon the bank's inclination to lend out its excess reserves. Suppose FDR Trust thought it should keep 25% as a reserve, even though the requirement was 20%. Then it would have lent out less money at each stage, and the money supply at the end would have been $400 instead of $500.

Third, the amount of expansion depends upon the amount of money people return to the banking system. If you had kept $20 in cash in your piggybank, then only $80 would have gone into bank reserves. The same would have been true if Mary had spent her loan at the hardware store, but the owner of the hardware store had put $20 in his piggybank.

Fourth, like Dumbo and his flying abilities, the system only works because you believe it does. If we all went to our banks and savings and loans and said, "please give me my money," it wouldn't be there. The bank has lent your money to someone else. If you have ever seen the movie *It's a Wonderful Life*, you will remember the scene where all of Jimmy Stewart's customers come into his savings and loan and demand their money at the same time. Jimmy tells them that he cannot give them their money because it has been loaned out to provide housing for all of them. Tom's money is over in Mary's house, and Joe's money is over in Tom's house. In a dramatic scene, Jimmy Stewart persuades his customers to take only what they need out of the savings and loan, and at the end of the day he has only two dollars left in the vault. Had Jimmy not been so persuasive, the savings and loan would have closed.

As I mentioned above, in 1933 (when this scene in *It's a Wonderful Life* takes place) there was a run on the banks and savings and loans. President Roosevelt shut the banks down and started federal deposit insurance. The purpose of federal deposit insurance is to keep you from asking for all of your money when your bank begins to get into trouble. The federal government guarantees you that your money, up to $100,000 at this time, will be paid to you even if your bank fails. Thus, you never worry that your money won't be there, and we don't all go down at once and ask for our money. Even so, if we did all ask for our money, the money would not be there. The federal deposit insurance corporation could never cover the amount of deposits that are not actually there. Just as Dumbo can fly as long as he believes he can fly, the banking system works as long as we all believe it works.

How Does the Government Affect the Money Supply?

The government can affect the money supply in a number of different ways. First, it can simply create currency, Federal Reserve notes, and coins.[63] The federal government by law has made Federal Reserve notes legal tender for all debts, public and private. This means that if someone owes you $100, you must take Federal Reserve notes as payment for the debt. The federal government also does not allow any of us to create our own money, for example Wyatt dollars redeemable for 1/300 of an ounce of gold and issued by my son. This means that government has a monopoly on the money supply. Since no one can create a competing money, the federal government can make each of its dollars worth less if it so chooses by making as many of them as it likes. This is handy for a government if it is a big debtor, since it may pay back dollars worth less than those that it borrowed.

The Federal Reserve has three other tools it may use to affect the money supply. It may increase or decrease the reserve requirement. When we looked at how banks create money we noticed that the amount of money created is affected by the reserve requirement. The smaller the reserve requirement, the greater the amount of money there will be for a given amount of reserves. The greater the reserve requirement, the smaller the amount of money there is for a given amount of reserves. As we noted above, for technical reasons the reserve requirement is not changed very often as a policy tool.

---

[63] Technically, federal statute requires that each Federal Reserve note be backed by a federal government security. However, this law could be changed as the debt held by the public declines.

Another tool is the discount rate. The Federal Reserve is a lender to banks, the so-called lender of last resort. If a bank has not kept enough reserves and does not have enough cash on hand to give people their deposits, the bank may borrow from the Federal Reserve. The interest rate that the Federal Reserve charges its banks is called the discount rate. The greater the discount rate, the more reserves banks are going to keep. This is because if it is very expensive to borrow from the Federal Reserve when I guess wrong about how many reserves to keep, then I will hold a little extra reserves. Rather than the 20% in our example, I might hold 25%, just in case one of my loans goes bad, or the timing of my loans doesn't fit the timing of withdrawals. The cheaper it is to borrow from the Federal Reserve, the more likely I am to lend out my excess reserves, as mistakes are more easily taken care of. Thus, the higher the discount rate, the greater the amount of excess reserves, and the smaller the money supply. The lower the discount rate, the less excess reserves, and the higher the money supply.

While the discount rate is changed fairly frequently, it often is changed as a response to market interest rates rather than a policy tool designed to influence the supply of money. As an example, if the Federal Reserve sets the discount rate at 4% and market interest rates move to 8%, then banks will be tempted to borrow from the Federal Reserve in order to profit from the difference in rates between what they can borrow at and what they can earn on the borrowings. So while it may appear that discount rate changes are used frequently to affect the money supply, they often are changed in response to market changes in interest rates.

The primary tool of the Federal Reserve is what is called open market operations. This is when the Federal Reserve buys and sells bonds. Suppose the Federal Reserve goes out into the open market and buys a $1000 government bond from Hillsdale County National Bank (HCNB). HCNB now has $1000 in additional reserves. This is because the Federal Reserve will either give HCNB $1000 in cash to add to HCNB's reserves, or it will credit HCNB's account with the Federal Reserve. In any event, HCNB now has additional reserves since the government bond it sold to the Federal Reserve did not count as reserves. Now that HCNB has excess reserves, it will loan some out. As it loans money out it creates checking accounts somewhere in the banking system, thus increasing the money supply as we discussed earlier in this chapter.

Suppose the Federal Reserve instead sold a $1000 bond to Hillsdale County National Bank. HCNB will give up $1000 in reserves in order to buy the bond, which does not count as reserves. When its reserves are reduced, HCNB can support fewer loans and thus fewer checking accounts. This reduces the money supply. Thus when the Federal Reserve sells bonds it reduces the money supply.

The Federal Reserve is in the money markets every day buying and selling bonds. The use of open market operations is the usual method the Federal Reserve uses when attempting to control reserves of banks and the money supply.

What Happens When the Government Changes the Amount of Money?

Let us briefly discuss the demand for money. You might think there is unlimited demand for money, but what you're really thinking is that there is an unlimited demand for wealth or income. Money is just one good in which we store our wealth or income before we buy something. When we speak of the demand for money, economists mean the demand for money given the amount of income or wealth you possess. Your demand for money is like the demand for any other good: it depends upon your income, preferences, and the price of other goods, in this case other assets like certificates of deposit or bonds. We can think of the price of money as the opportunity cost of holding it, which is what you could have earned had you bought a bond or other financial asset. This is the interest rate. And like any other good, when the price of money (interest rate) rises, the quantity demanded goes down, and when the price (interest rate) falls the quantity demanded goes up.

Just as for any other good, demand and supply determine the equilibrium price of money. If the supply of money increases, the equilibrium price of money, the interest rate, will fall as long as the demand does not shift. Thus interest rates will fall when government increases the money supply.

Despite what we have just theorized, we may witness the market interest rate rising when the government increases the money supply. There are a number of reasons why this occurs. First, remember when we put the price of something on a demand and supply schedule, it is understood that this is the relative price; that is, it is the price of the good relative to other goods. When there is inflation it introduces "noise" into the system. We cannot tell if the price of a good is going up because the value of money is falling, and thus all goods are increasing in value, or if the demand for this good has gone up so its relative price has increased. In the case of interest rates, we also have a "noise" problem. The interest rate in the demand and supply for money is a relative price. When inflation happens, the market nominal interest rate will rise to reflect inflation's effect on the value of money. The point is that if the Federal Reserve increases the money supply, and thereby causes inflation, market interest rates may increase to reflect the fact that the dollar is worth less, and thus only the "real" interest rate declines. This would be the interest rate that takes account of the inflation.

Second, people may get worried about what is going to happen to inflation, and build a "risk" factor into what they want to receive to lend you money. This would actually increase "real" interest rates, because of people's response to the government's policy to increase the money supply.

In any event, the standard Keynesian model has interest rates declining when the supply of money increases. Recall from Chapter 14 that investment demand, one of the major components of aggregate demand, depends on the interest rate. The higher the interest rate, the less likely people are to put their money into a drill press, and the more likely they are to buy a bond with it, or put it into a certificate of deposit, or other financial asset. The lower the interest rate, the more likely they are to put the money into a drill press which will help earn extra profit. Firms will invest, that is purchase machinery and buildings and add to their inventories, when the added profit from doing so exceeds the rate of interest. In this way, investment declines when interest rates rise and investment increases when interest rates fall.

Following this train of thought, the connection between monetary policy and changes in GDP is through the interest rate. If the government wants to reduce unemployment, the Federal Reserve will buy bonds. This will increase the reserves of banks. Banks will increase their loans, thus creating more checking accounts thereby increasing the supply of money. The increase in the supply of money reduces interest rates. Reducing interest rates increases investment demand. Increasing investment demand increases aggregate demand. The increase in aggregate demand increases equilibrium GDP, thus reducing unemployment.

By now you must be thinking, "this is pretty complicated." How does the Federal Reserve know how much to increase the money supply to get to the correct equilibrium GDP? How long does it take for this process to work itself out? What if the banks don't want to loan out these excess reserves? There are a number of questions that readily come to mind. The answers don't come to mind quite as easily.

Milton Friedman basically says that even if monetary policy worked in the way the Keynesian model has it work, no one can really know the answer to most of the above questions. Thus, the Federal Reserve is just as likely, probably more likely, to make things worse as they are to make things better. Friedman has for years recommended that the Federal Reserve just try to keep money supply growth at a constant level. There are other theories, such as the rational expectations school, that lead to the same conclusion. This is not the forum to discuss the pros and cons of the various theories of fiscal and monetary policy. But you should know that there are plenty of economists (as well as others) who do not subscribe to the Keynesian model. Many of these believe that the fiscal policy and monetary policy prescriptions of the Keynesian model do no good and are more likely to do harm than to be simply ineffective.

Should Government Have a Monopoly on Money?

In the last chapter we noted that Keynesian fiscal policy prescriptions totally bypass the larger political- economy question of the proper role of government in society. The same has been true of Keynesian monetary policy, as well as most of the critics of Keynesian policies. There have been a few who have questioned whether government should have a monopoly over the good we call money. Some that come to mind include Hans Sennholz, Murray Rothbard, and Friedrich Hayek. For the most part, however, the question of the right of a government to monopolize the currency never comes up.

We do not give government a monopoly over the production of food, so why should we accept without question that we should give it a monopoly over money? There is one reason government would like to have monopoly control over the money supply, and that is because it allows the government to tax you through inflation.

To see how this can happen, let us recall the story of Jack and the Beanstalk. Remember that Jack and his mother live in a small village and are very poor. Jack goes to town to sell the cow and receives in payment some magic beans. These beans grow into a beanstalk leading up to a giant's castle. Jack climbs the beanstalk, and, to make a fairy tale short, Jack steals the hen that lays golden eggs. From our perspective the real story now begins. We are told that Jack and his mother will no longer be poor because they have a vast supply of golden eggs. Gold evidently can be used as money in their village and, at first glance, it appears all will live happily ever after.

Let's examine why Jack and his mother are richer. Jack is producing nothing more than golden eggs. Thus, the village seems to have the same amount of people, and the same amount of "stuff." Unless golden eggs have some use other than for money, the village as a whole is no richer. It simply has more money. Since there is more money and the same amount of other goods, the value of money will fall. Once the number of golden eggs has increased, it will take more gold to buy bacon, or bread, or milk than it did before. This is inflation. Jack's goose will simply create inflation because it has created more money but has not added to production, thus reducing the value of money.

That might be the end of it. The village is as poor as it was, there is just more of the local currency. The same amount of goods would be there, and the prices of everything would be higher. However, there will be a redistribution of wealth. Since Jack gets the eggs before anyone else, he is able to buy what he wants before the prices start to rise. When he walks into town with the first golden egg, the person selling the milk will no doubt sell the milk at a price that reflects the initial amount of gold in the village. So Jack gets the milk.

Now at the end of the day, when Old Mother Hubbard comes to the store, the milk is all gone. The storekeeper, seeing an excess demand for his goods, raises his price for milk. As the price of milk rises, Old Mother Hubbard, who is on a fixed pension left to her by the late Old Father Hubbard, cannot buy as much milk as before.

This happens for all goods. Jack's increased demand has led to an increase in prices. But since Jack is always the one to get the new money first, he ends up with more of the goods. The ability of Jack to produce money has allowed him to obtain goods without producing other new goods.

This is basically how the government obtains resources when it uses inflation as a taxing mechanism. Think of the government as owning the hen that lays the golden eggs. When it wants to have a bridge built, it can write checks to contractors, asphalt manufacturers, etc., and obtain these resources before the new money it creates drives up prices. Since the government always has the new money first, it gets people to swap their stuff for money, which by the end of the chain, has become worth significantly less. The people who are taxed the most in this system are those who are last in the chain. These are people whose income doesn't respond very quickly to inflation, or people who have saved.

Imagine that you lived in Jack's village and had stored away 100 ounces of gold before the golden eggs came into the village. That 100 ounces of gold could have purchased a certain amount of goods. After Jack increased the amount of gold in the village, your 100 ounces, however, will purchase less than it did before Jack started adding to the money supply. In effect, Jack's action taxed away some of your savings. The same thing happened to senior citizens during the late 1970's in the United States when inflation rates neared 15%. The value of the savings of senior citizens declined, or was taxed away by the government's increase of the money supply.

One problem with allowing the government to have a monopoly over the economy's money is that there is always an incentive for the government to tax us through inflation. It is a tax that does not need voter or even Congressional, approval. This, of course, has been well known for many years, especially among economists. But the average citizen is unlikely to know how this all works, and thus is less likely to punish his own congressman for this type of tax than for a direct tax. Thus, governments worldwide jealously guard their monopoly over the money of their country.[64]

Private Money

Should we have private money? As noted above, there are those who think it wouldn't be such a bad idea. For decades, private money existed in the United States. The period between the second bank of the United States and the Federal Reserve was one such period. From 1839 to 1913, much of the money supply consisted of privately issued bank notes. Real personal income growth during this

---

[64] Buchanan and Wagner offer an explanation of why democracies are likely to use this method of financing government expenditures in *Democracy in Deficit: the Political Legacy of Lord Keynes* cited above. The mechanism through which we are taxed is a little more complicated than with Jack and the Beanstalk, but the basic principle is the same.

period was faster than it has been since the establishment of the Federal Reserve. This is not to say everything went smoothly. Banking "panics" ensued every twenty years or so, and some persons found that the banks had issued notes which eventually became worth much less than their face value. However, individuals had a choice of what currency to use, and good currencies, backed by a stable commodity such as gold, would drive out bad currencies. It is possible that such a system could work today.

It is not the purpose of this text to either detail how such a system would work, or to argue for or against private currency. Hans Sennholz's little book, *Money and Freedom*,[65] is a good place to start for those who wish to pursue the matter. The purpose is, as has been pointed out through the various chapters, to start you thinking. It is easy to simply assume that government should have a monopoly over the money commodity, since that is the case in most countries throughout the world. But it is important to ask whether this need be the case, and if not, whether it ought to be the case.

In answering whether it ought to be the case is not simply a question of what is the most expedient method of organizing a currency. One should also ask as Bastiat would, is a law limiting currency to government money alone a just law? Would Mises or Hayek consider legal tender laws consistent with a free society? These questions are not simply academic exercises. As Europe struggles with monetary and economic union, these are the type of questions which should be asked, but will most likely be overlooked. When discussions of monetary policy take place, the basic notion of the proper role of government in the economy is seldom even discussed. Even when discussing the political independence of central banks, the focus seldom turns to the basic questions.

---

[65] (Spring Mills, Pa: Libertarian Press, Inc., 1985). See also, Murray Rothbard's *What Has Government Done to our Money?* (San Rafael, Ca: Libertarian Publishers, 1985).

Chapter 16

THE INDIVIDUAL, THE MARKET SYSTEM, AND SOCIETY

As you may have now realized, political economy is really a study of the social order. Having moved through the chapters of this book you should now understand how society organizes its resources under a market system, a system based upon cooperating individuals with specialization of labor and voluntary exchange as the foundation for interaction. The market system is not only the most efficient system of using and developing resources, it is the only system that works in the sense of providing an increasing standard of living. The information problem and the incentive problem of modern society cannot be solved through a planned economy. The fall of Eastern Europe's planned economies is simply confirmation of what Mises pointed out in the early part of the 20th century.

We have learned that not only is the market system the most efficient, and in the long run, the only viable one, it is also the only social order consistent with individual liberty. It is impossible to separate the basic freedom to choose what you will do with your time and resources from political freedom. While for some of us individual freedom is something to be sought for its own sake, Hayek has taught us that individual liberty and the responsibility that goes along with it create the most efficient use of knowledge and the most productive society.

Capitalism and the market order leads to a just society when justice is defined as Bastiat has suggested: there is a role for government, and this role is an extension of our natural right to self-defense. Governments that concentrate on protecting the individual from threats by other members of society and do not use coercive force to take from one member of society to give to another are "just" governments. Looking at our urban centers in today's United States, it is apparent that governments have forgotten their primary role. This has contributed to the breakdown of the social order and the economic decline of our great cities. Those with a desire to find solutions to our urban problems would do well to keep in mind the words of Bastiat and others who have thought deeply about the role of government in society.

A market order is one in which people have the ability and the responsibility to practice true philanthropy. Our discussions of Bastiat and Hayek should make you think about what it means to be truly philanthropic. Only in a society where you own your own resources are you able to truly give of yourself and your resources. The good Samaritan did not simply fill out his 1040 long form and rely on government to take care of the injured traveler.

The history of Western civilization demonstrates conclusively that a social order based upon individual freedom and responsibility, with as little coercion as possible, has led to the vast improvement in the standard of living of everyone in Western society. Innovation drives economic advancement, and innovation is fostered by the market system of rewards and responsibilities. Any country wishing to improve the living conditions of its citizenry need only look to the history of capitalist society for answers.

The United States enters the twenty-first century with a government that has grown to an annual budget of more than $1.8 trillion, a national debt of more than $5.5 trillion, federal regulations that no one, not even the regulators, can keep track of, and a deteriorating moral order in its urban society where people are afraid to walk the streets in broad daylight.

We must begin to search for answers to our problems, not in macroeconomic models of the economy, nor in bigger government, but in the workings of a free society and in the writings of those who asked the basic questions. As the Swiss parapsychologist Carl Jung once said, "Understanding does not cure evil, but it is a definite help, inasmuch as one can cope with a comprehensible darkness." Much of the problem of today's society comes about from a misplaced distrust of the individual's capacity for goodness. When we understand how individuals interact in a truly free society, we will begin to solve a number of the problems of modern society. The fall of the statist societies of Eastern Europe provides enormous opportunity for everyone, including those already living in market economies. We can learn from their failure. We must recognize where we are headed and what we are capable of as free, responsible individuals. But this can only happen when we first understand what it actually means to be a free society.